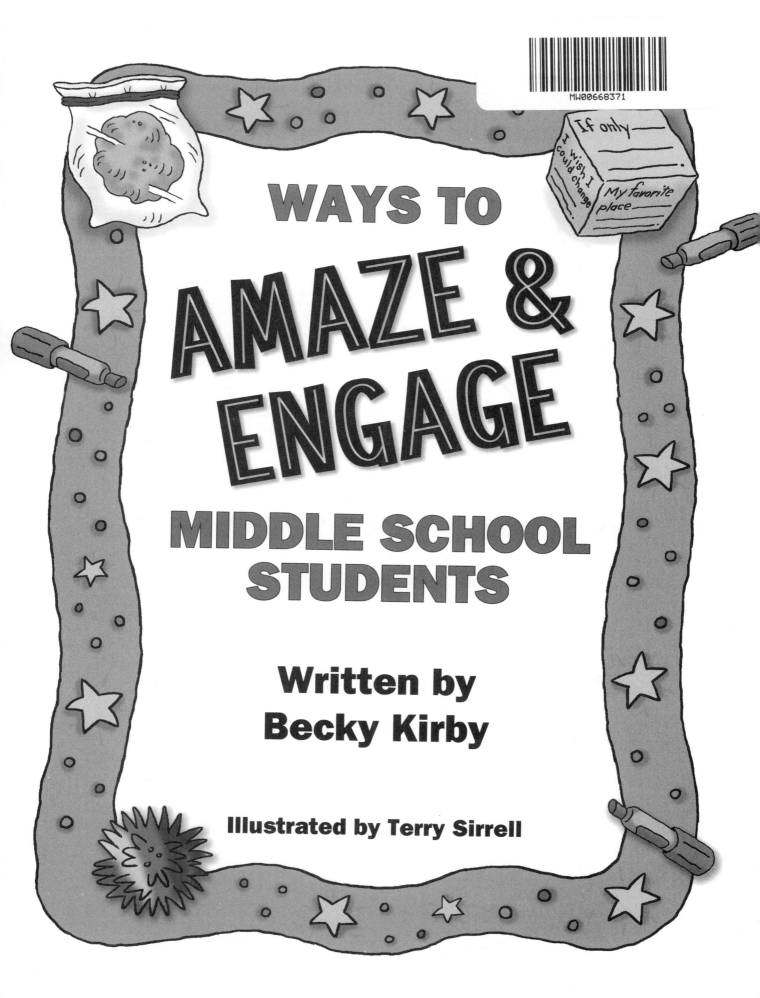

WAYS TO AMAZE & ENGAGE

MIDDLE SCHOOL STUDENTS

Written by Becky Kirby

Illustrated by Terry Sirrell

Ways To Amaze And Engage Middle School Students

10-DIGIT ISBN: 1-57543-173-4
13-DIGIT ISBN: 978-1-57543-173-4

COPYRIGHT © 2009 MAR∗CO PRODUCTS, INC.
Published by mar∗co products, inc.
1443 Old York Road
Warminster, PA 18974
1-800-448-2197
www.marcoproducts.com

PRINTED IN THE U.S.A.

Dedication

I dedicate this book to my husband, David, who has been very supportive during the writing of all three of my books. We often make the 12-hour drive between Hilton Head Island, SC and our home in Ohio. I do some of my best writing while David is behind the wheel. I appreciate him.

I also dedicate this book to my parents Jane and Art Fesemyer. My dad was an English teacher when I was young. In the summer, when friends were outside playing, my sisters and I were in the house reading and writing the book reports our father required of us. At the time, I dreaded his reviews and corrections, but now I appreciate that these exercises helped develop my love of reading, writing, and the English language.

Lastly, I dedicate this book to my new grandsons. Kyle David Kirby was born in March 2008 to my son Greg and his wife Michelle. Mason Charles Ratliff was born in July 2006 in Wuhan, in the Chinese province of Hubei. He joined the family of my daughter Kristine, her husband, Charles, and their daughter Maggie on November 11, 2008.

Table Of Contents

Introduction

Our elementary school library contained a book titled *Make It Take It*. Although not a particularly creative or artistic child, I could easily complete the projects described in this book. I sometimes marveled at the end results.

I hope that *Ways To Amaze And Engage Middle School Students* is the *Make It Take It* book for school counselors. Most of its lessons are easy for counselors to prepare and present, and students have fun while learning. This book is a compilation of activities I most enjoy using with middle school students, and most of the activities can be adapted for elementary and high school students.

The activities are grouped in two ways. The Table Of Contents lists activities under the topic that best fits how they are presented. In the Topic Index at the end of the book, activities are listed under their respective topics.

I hope you find the activities effective and motivating for your students. I hope that you and your students marvel at the end results.

Becky Kirby

Instructions For Using The CD

The CD found inside the back cover provides ADOBE® PDF files of each lesson's reproducible pages.

For example: *Waystoamaze_018.pdf* is the same as page 18 in the book.

The PDF files are provided in color or black and white. The color pages may be printed in black and white. Choose the appropriate setting on your computer.

These files cannot be modified/edited.

System requirements to open PDF (.pdf) files:

Adobe Reader® 5.0 or newer (compatible with Windows 2000® or newer or Mac OS 9.0® or newer).

This CD may not be duplicated or distributed.

PERMISSION TO REPRODUCE: The purchaser may reproduce the activity sheets, free and without special permission, for participant use for a particular group or class. Sharing these files with other counselors/faculty members or reproduction of these materials for an entire school system is forbidden.

SMALL-GROUP ACTIVITIES

Best/Worst

Purpose:

To help students express their feelings about given situations

Materials:

For each student:
- ☐ *The Best And The Worst* (page 13 or CD-Rom)
- ☐ Pencil or pen

ASCA Standards:

PERSONAL/SOCIAL DEVELOPMENT	
Standard A: Students will acquire the knowledge, attitudes and interpersonal skills to help them understand and respect self and others.	
PS:A1	Acquire Self-Knowledge
PS:A1.5	Identify and express feelings
PS:A2	Acquire Interpersonal Skills
PS:A2.2	Respect alternative points of view

Directions:

On a copy of *The Best And The Worst,* have each student list the best and worst aspects of a selected situation. A variation is the *Easiest/Hardest.* Some examples of situations are:

- this school year
- your friends
- the cafeteria
- vacation
- homework
- parents' divorce (divorce-group activity)

- your family
- today's weather
- school clubs and sports
- tests
- the world situation

Be creative. Students may write on any selected topic. When the allotted time has elapsed, have the students share what they have written.

Ways To Amaze And Engage Middle School Students © 2009 Mar⋆co Products, Inc. 1.800.448.2197

THE BEST AND THE WORST

TOPIC:

BEST/EASIEST	WORST/HARDEST

Cube

Purpose:

To allow the counselor to get the know students better and to have students share their feelings

Materials:

For the leader:
- ☐ An empty mug-size box
- ☐ Markers

ASCA Standards:

PERSONAL/SOCIAL DEVELOPMENT	
Standard A: Students will acquire the knowledge, attitudes and interpersonal skills to help them understand and respect self and others.	
PS:A1	Acquire Self-Knowledge
PS:A1.2	Identify values, attitudes and beliefs

Directions:

Write open-ended sentences on each side of the empty box. Some examples of open-ended sentences are:

- If only _____ .
- The best thing that could happen _____ .
- The hardest thing I've ever done _____ .
- My favorite place_____ .
- If I could meet anyone, I'd like to meet _____ .
- I wish I could change _____ .

The students take turns tossing the cube. When the cube lands, the students complete the open-ended sentence facing them.

This activity may be performed with an entire class or in small groups. There should be one cube for each group. The students take turns tossing the cube and talking with other group members.

Ways To Amaze And Engage Middle School Students © 2009 Mar∗co Products, Inc. 1.800.448.2197

A final activity consists of having the students choose which statement they want to discuss in more detail.

Variation:

Write a different *feeling word* on each side of the box. Have the students describe a time they experienced the feeling the word describes.

Ways To Amaze And Engage Middle School Students © 2009 Mar∗co Products, Inc. 1.800.448.2197

Family Picture

Purpose:

To enable the counselor to learn more about a student and his/her family dynamics

Materials:

For the leader:
☐ Board or chart paper and marker

For each student:
☐ Drawing paper
☐ Pen or pencil
☐ *Feeling Words* (page 18 or CD-Rom)

ASCA Standards:

PERSONAL/SOCIAL DEVELOPMENT	
Standard A: Students will acquire the knowledge, attitudes and interpersonal skills to help them understand and respect self and others.	
PS:A1	Acquire Self-Knowledge
PS:A1.11	Identify and discuss changing personal and social roles
PS:A1.12	Identify and recognize changing family roles
PS:A2	Acquire Interpersonal Skills
PS:A2.5	Recognize and respect differences in various family configurations

Directions:

Asking students to draw a family picture promotes discussion and provides insight about each student's family relationships. This is especially effective for individual and group counseling.

To show what a family picture might look like, draw the example on page 17 on the board or chart paper.

Ways To Amaze And Engage Middle School Students © 2009 Mar✶co Products, Inc. 1.800.448.2197

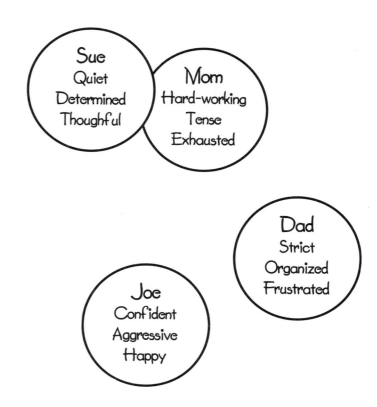

Using the example, ask the students about Sue's relationship with Mom and Joe's relationship with Dad. Have them explain why the student in the example may have distanced him/herself from the family.

Ask each student to use circles to draw his/her family and mark each circle with the initials or name of the person that circle represents. Circles representing people who are close to one another should be drawn close together. Circles representing people who are not close to one another should be drawn far apart. After the students have completed their drawings, give each student a copy of *Feeling Words.* Ask the students to write three words that describe their mom, three words that describe their dad, and three words that describe themselves. (You may have to vary this for individual students, using *guardian, step-parent,* etc.) The students may choose words from the *Feeling Words* worksheet or write their own feeling-word descriptions. (*Note:* You may also include siblings.) Have the students share their pictures with the group, telling why they placed circles where they did and why they described family members the way they did. Use the students' answers to promote discussion.

Ways To Amaze And Engage Middle School Students © 2009 Mar✷co Products, Inc. 1.800.448.2197

FEELING WORDS

Afraid
Aggressive
Annoyed
Anxious
Blissful
Bored
Calm
Caring
Concerned
Confident
Confused
Content
Depressed
Determined
Disappointed
Discouraged
Disgusted
Enraged
Excited
Exhausted
Fearful
Frustrated
Gloomy
Guilty
Happy

Heartbroken
Hopeful
Hurt
Infuriated
Irritated
Lonely
Mad
Miserable
Pained
Panicky
Proud
Quiet
Regretful
Sad
Satisfied
Scared
Shy
Strict
Tense
Terrific
Terrified
Thoughtful
Uneasy
Wonderful
Worried

Grief Letter/Journal

Purpose:

To show students you care about their loss

Materials:

For the leader:
- ☐ Colored or textured paper

For each student:
- ☐ Journal
- ☐ Pen
- ☐ *Grief Letter* (page 20 or CD-Rom)

ASCA Standards:

PERSONAL/SOCIAL DEVELOPMENT	
Standard C: Students will understand safety and survival skills.	
PS:C1	Acquire Personal Safety Skills
PS:C1.11	Learn coping skills for managing life events

Directions:

The holiday season can be a particularly difficult time for a student who has lost a loved one. Giving each bereaved student a copy of the *Grief Letter* and a journal acknowledges the loss and lets him/her know you care.

Copying the letter on colored or textured paper is a nice touch. It can be retyped and personalized to state the student's relationship with the person who has died. Along with the letter, present a journal in which the student can write about his/her loved one.

Date _____

Dear_____ ,

The holiday season can be a difficult time for someone who has lost a loved one. It is my wish this holiday season that you use this journal to help you focus on memories of your loved one. Write about your pain and your courage and about how you are confronting your sorrow. Write about the person or people to whom you're reaching out and about who is reaching out to you. Write about the good and happy times you shared with the person who has died. Write about the times you laughed together and the times you cried, the times you were angry with each other, the silly things you did together, and the caring and joy you gave each other. Write about your love for this person and the love he/she had for you. During this holiday season, focus on your memories and the love you shared.

Sincerely,

Jellyroll Hug

Purpose:

To build group cohesion

Materials:

None required

ASCA Standards:

PERSONAL/SOCIAL DEVELOPMENT	
Standard A: Students will acquire the knowledge, attitudes and interpersonal skills to help them understand and respect self and others.	
PS:A1	Acquire Self-Knowledge
PS:A1.9	Demonstrate cooperative behavior in groups

Directions:

A jellyroll hug is a good way to end a final group or class session. Dividing a class into two or more groups enables students to maneuver more easily.

Have the students stand shoulder to shoulder in a straight line and put their arms around the waists of the people next to them. Have the student on one end of the line begin to walk toward the others in a circular way. The other students follow slowly, turning in like a jellyroll being made. The first person will be in the middle of the circle. Once everyone is in the circle, the students stand still, count to 3, then squeeze with a big hug.

(*Note*: You may want to put a student who needs positive attention on the end of the line, so he/she will end up in the middle.)

Ways To Amaze And Engage Middle School Students © 2009 Mar✶co Products, Inc. 1.800.448.2197

Memory Box

Purpose:

To teach students to recognize positive traits in others

Materials:

For the leader:
- ☐ Scissors
- ☐ Scrapbooking paper of various patterns. Each student should have a strip about 8″ long and 1″ wide for each classmate.

For each student:
- ☐ Shoe box, small box, or lidded jar
- ☐ Pencil
- ☐ Markers or crayons

ASCA Standards:

PERSONAL/SOCIAL DEVELOPMENT	
Standard A: Students will acquire the knowledge, attitudes and interpersonal skills to help them understand and respect self and others.	
PS:A2	Acquire Interpersonal Skills
PS:A2.3	Recognize, accept, respect and appreciate individual differences

Directions:

(*Note:* This activity is good at a final group session or, with a class, at the end of the school year.)

Tell the students they will be making a *Memory Box.* Allow time for them to decorate the outside of their box or jar.

Give each student one strip of paper for each person in the group/class.

Featuring one student at a time, have each student write something positive about him/her on the blank side of the paper.

Ways To Amaze And Engage Middle School Students © 2009 Mar∗co Products, Inc. 1.800.448.2197

After the students have written their notes, tell them to roll the strip tightly around a pencil so it forms a curl or spiral. The outside of the strip should be the decorative side of the scrapbooking paper.

Give the completed notes to each featured student to put into his/her Memory Box.

When everyone has finished, every student's box will be filled with positive messages from classmates.

Ways To Amaze And Engage Middle School Students © 2009 Mar*co Products, Inc. 1.800.448.2197

PlayDough® Stress Ball

Purpose:

To have the students make a stress-management tool

ASCA Standards:

PERSONAL/SOCIAL DEVELOPMENT	
Standard C: Students will understand safety and survival skills.	
PS:C1	Acquire Personal Safety Skills
PS:C1.11	Learn coping skills for managing life events

Directions:

Gather the students around a table on which the materials have been placed. Tell them to measure 1 cup of flour, ½ cup of salt, and ½ cup of water into each bowl, then knead the ingredients until they form a ball. If using food coloring, add it now. If the mixture is too sticky, add flour. If the mixture is too dry, add a little water. Have each student place the mixture in a small plastic bag.

Tell the students to keep their stress balls nearby so they can relieve their stress by squeezing the dough in the plastic bag.

Puzzles

Purpose:

To involve students in a cooperative group activity

ASCA Standards:

PERSONAL/SOCIAL DEVELOPMENT	
Standard A: Students will acquire the knowledge, attitudes and interpersonal skills to help them understand and respect self and others.	
PS:A1	Acquire Self-Knowledge
PS:A1.9	Demonstrate cooperative behavior in groups

Directions:

Divide the students into groups. Give each group member one or more pieces of the puzzle. Tell the students to work together, without talking, to put the puzzle together.

When all the puzzles have been completed, ask:

- How did you communicate?
- What was hard about this activity?
- What was easy about this activity?
- Did everyone work together to complete the puzzle?
- Did someone in your group act as a leader?
- What roles did group members take?

 ☆ 25 ☆

PUZZLE TEMPLATE 2

PUZZLE TEMPLATE 4

CLASSROOM ACTIVITIES

Ball Toss

Purpose:

To have students get to know each other

Materials:

For each student:
- ☐ *Ball Toss* (page 33 or CD-Rom)
- ☐ Pencil

ASCA Standards:

PERSONAL/SOCIAL DEVELOPMENT	
Standard A: Students will acquire the knowledge, attitudes and interpersonal skills to help them understand and respect self and others.	
PS:A2	Acquire Interpersonal Skills
PS:A2.3	Recognize, accept, respect and appreciate individual differences

Directions:

Tell the students to answer the questions on the activity sheet, but not to write their names on it.

Have the students wad the paper into a ball when they have finished.

When everyone is ready, have the students throw the balls back and forth until you tell them to stop. Tell them not to throw hard and not to hit anyone above the shoulders.

After a pre-determined amount of time, tell the students to stop, pick up a ball, and sit down.

Taking turns, each student reads the answers to the questions on the activity sheet and tries to guess whose paper it is.

Ways To Amaze And Engage Middle School Students © 2009 Mar✳co Products, Inc. 1.800.448.2197

BALL TOSS

Write your answers to the following questions:

If someone called you right now, who would you want it to be?

_____

_____

_____

What is your favorite thing to do?

_____

_____

_____

Whom do you admire?

_____

_____

_____

What is the best thing that could happen to you right now?

_____

_____

_____

Ways To Amaze And Engage Middle School Students © 2009 Mar∗co Products, Inc. 1.800.448.2197

Beach Ball

Purpose:

To teach stress-management techniques

Materials:

For the leader:
- ☐ Beach ball or other large, bouncy ball
- ☐ Permanent marker
- ☐ Optional: Masking tape

ASCA Standards:

PERSONAL/SOCIAL DEVELOPMENT	
Standard C: Students will understand safety and survival skills.	
PS:C1	Acquire Personal Safety Skills
PS:C1.10	Learn techniques for managing stress and conflict

Directions:

With a permanent marker, write on the ball different things that cause stress. Or write on strips of masking tape and stick them all over the ball.

Suggested situations are:

- moving to a new school
- parents' divorce
- loss
- choosing sides for a team
- winning an award
- illness
- new pet
- sports
- new situations

- state tests
- grades
- exclusion
- being in the school play
- friends
- sibling moving away
- homework
- gym class

Have the students stand in a circle. Explain that the ball will be thrown to different class members.

Ways To Amaze And Engage Middle School Students © 2009 Mar∗co Products, Inc. 1.800.448.2197

A student who catches the ball reads the stressful situation closest to his/her right thumb. He/she tells why, how, or when, this situation may be stressful and what he/she could do to relieve stress.

Each class member should have a turn. If the ball is thrown to a class member who has already had a turn, he/she should throw the ball to a classmate who hasn't had a turn.

The teacher/counselor begins the activity by throwing the ball to the first person.

When everyone has had a turn, ask the students if anything positive can result from stress.

Variation:

Assign a topic that can cause stress to each color on the beach ball. For example:

- Red—School
- Green—Home/Family
- White—Relationships
- Yellow—World Affairs
- Blue—Extracurricular Activities

Throw the ball. The student who catches the ball looks at the color his/her right thumb touches, compares the color to the assigned stress topic, and explains how that topic can be stressful and what can be done to relieve the stress.

Ways To Amaze And Engage Middle School Students © 2009 Mar∗co Products, Inc. 1.800.448.2197

Brag Bag

Purpose:

To give and receive positive messages

ASCA Standards:

PERSONAL/SOCIAL DEVELOPMENT	
Standard A: Students will acquire the knowledge, attitudes and interpersonal skills to help them understand and respect self and others.	
PS:A2	Acquire Interpersonal Skills
PS:A2.3	Recognize, accept, respect and appreciate individual differences

Materials:

For the leader:
- ☐ *Brag Bag Form* (page 38 or CD-Rom)
- ☐ Tape

For each student:
- ☐ Paper lunch bag
- ☐ Colored markers

Directions:

Have the students decorate the lunch bags and put their names on them.

Tape the bags around the classroom.

Show the students the *Brag Bag Form*. Explain that each day, they are to write something positive to someone in the class and put the paper in that person's bag. They must choose a different person each day.

Once every student has written about every other student, the bags may be returned to their owners. Ask the students to share some positive comments written to them.

(*Note:* When the students are not in the room, the teacher may want to make sure all comments are appropriate.)

Ways To Amaze And Engage Middle School Students © 2009 Mar✳co Products, Inc. 1.800.448.2197

Conclude the lesson by having the students respond to the following questions:

- How did it feel to write something positive to someone?
- How does it feel to read the positive messages that people wrote to you?
- How does it feel to hear others read the positive messages that people wrote about them?

Variation:

Feature a different student each day. Classmates write something positive about the featured student. Continue until everyone has been the featured student.

BRAG BAG FORM

This Positive Message is for: _____

From: _____

_____

_____

_____

_____

_____

#1

BRAG BAG FORM

This Positive Message is for: _____

From: _____

_____

_____

_____

_____

_____

#1

☆ 38 ☆

Brag Ball

Purpose:

To help students develop a positive attitude toward themselves and others

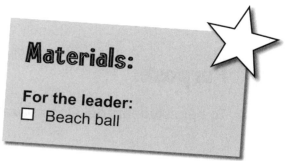

Materials:

For the leader:
☐ Beach ball

ASCA Standards:

PERSONAL/SOCIAL DEVELOPMENT	
Standard A: Students will acquire the knowledge, attitudes and interpersonal skills to help them understand and respect self and others.	
PS:A1	Acquire Self-Knowledge
PS:A1.1	Develop positive attitudes toward self as a unique and worthy person

Directions:

Have the students stand in a circle.

The beach ball will be passed from student to student around the circle. The student holding the ball is to brag about him/herself or his/her friends or family.

The teacher/counselor models this activity, then passes the beach ball to the left.

Variation:

If time permits, students could brag about themselves for the first round, about friends for the second round, and about family for the third round.

Ways To Amaze And Engage Middle School Students © 2009 Mar∗co Products, Inc. 1.800.448.2197

Bubbles

Purpose:

To help students develop relaxation strategies

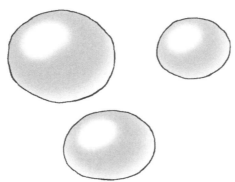

Materials:

For the leader:
☐ Several bottles of bubble solution (unless providing one bottle for each student)

For each student group:
☐ Paper plate or bowl
☐ Bubble solution

For each student:
☐ Bubble wand

ASCA Standards:

PERSONAL/SOCIAL DEVELOPMENT	
Standard C: Students will understand safety and survival skills.	
PS:C1	Acquire Personal Safety Skills
PS:C1.10	Learn techniques for managing stress and conflict
PS:C1.11	Learn coping skills for managing life events

Directions:

Review relaxation techniques. Some ideas are deep breathing, visualization, journaling, and exercising.

Tell the students that another way to relax is to blow bubbles and that they'll be blowing their stress away with bubbles.

Give each student a bubble wand. (*Note:* Fancy wands that blow a lot of bubbles at once are best, but regular ones will work.) Or give each student a small bottle of bubble solution that includes a wand.

Divide the students into groups of four. Give each group a paper plate/bowl and bubble solution.

Tell the students to think of things that are stressing them, dip their wands in the solution, and blow their stress away. Bubbles will float throughout the room.

Remind the students to focus on slow, deep breathing as they blow their stress away.

When the allotted time has elapsed, have the students describe how it felt to blow their stress away.

Allow students who wish to do so to share the stresses they blew away.

Ways To Amaze And Engage Middle School Students © 2009 Mar*co Products, Inc. 1.800.448.2197

All About You Catcher

Purpose:

To help students develop positive attitudes about themselves

Materials:

For each student:
- ☐ *All About You Catcher* (page 44 or CD-Rom)
- ☐ Scissors
- ☐ Optional: Crayons or markers

ASCA Standards:

PERSONAL/SOCIAL DEVELOPMENT	
Standard A: Students will acquire the knowledge, attitudes and interpersonal skills to help them understand and respect self and others.	
PS:A1	Acquire Self-Knowledge
PS:A1.1	Develop positive attitudes toward self as a unique and worthy person

Directions:

1. Cut out the *All About You Catcher* square.
2. Optional: Color the squares.
3. Turn the catcher so the blank side is on top.
4. Fold each corner toward the center.
5. Turn the square over and fold each corner toward the center, with colors on top.
6. Fold this in half, so numbers show on top.
7. Fold it in half again, with numbers showing.
8. Open the square slightly and slip your fingers into the openings.
9. Slip your left thumb under the 1, 2 slot and your left pointer finger under the 7, 8 slot.
   or
   Slip your right thumb finger under the 3, 4 slot and your right pointer finger under the 5, 6 slot.
10. With the points toward the center, practice opening and closing the catcher.

11. Choose a partner. Have your partner choose a number between *1* and *8*. Open and close the catcher that many times, ending with it open.
12. Ask your partner to choose a color.
13. Open the colored section and read the question. Have your partner answer it.
14. Now it is your partner's turn to ask the questions and open and close the catcher.

ALL ABOUT YOU
Catcher

- When is the last time you laughed so hard you cried?
- If you could only see one color, what color would you choose?
- What is your best quality?
- Where is your favorite place?
- What is your idea of a perfect day?
- How old would you like to be?
- What is the best thing that could happen to you?
- Who would you like to spend a day with?

RED · GREEN · YELLOW · BLUE · PINK · ORANGE · BLACK · PURPLE

1 2 3 4 5 6 7 8

Ways To Amaze And Engage Middle School Students © 2009 Mar✶co Products, Inc. 1.800.448.2197

Ways To Say "No" Catcher

Purpose:

To teach or review strategies for saying "no" when dealing with peer pressure

Materials:

For each student:
- [ ] *Ways to Say "No" Catcher* (page 46 or CD-Rom)
- [ ] Scissors
- [ ] Optional: Crayons or markers

ASCA Standards:

PERSONAL/SOCIAL DEVELOPMENT	
Standard C: Students will understand safety and survival skills.	
PS:C1	Acquire Personal Safety Skills
PS:C1.9	Learn how to cope with peer pressure

Directions:

Follow the *All About You Catcher directions on pages 42-43.*

Ways To Amaze And Engage Middle School Students © 2009 Mar*co Products, Inc. 1.800.448.2197

WAYS TO SAY "NO"
Catcher

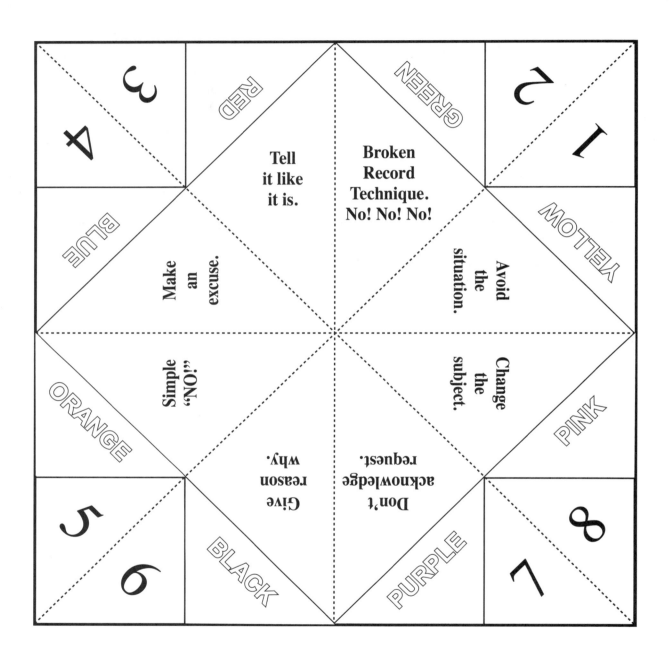

Tell it like it is.

Broken Record Technique. No! No! No!

Make an excuse.

Avoid the situation.

Simple "NO!"

Change the subject.

Give reason why.

Don't acknowledge request.

RED · GREEN · YELLOW · PINK · PURPLE · BLACK · ORANGE · BLUE

1 · 2 · 3 · 4 · 5 · 6 · 7 · 8

Stress Catcher

Purpose:

To teach or review stress-management techniques

Materials:

For each student:
- ☐ *Stress Catcher* (page 48 or CD-Rom)
- ☐ Scissors
- ☐ Optional: Crayons or markers

ASCA Standards:

PERSONAL/SOCIAL DEVELOPMENT	
Standard C: Students will understand safety and survival skills.	
PS:C1	Acquire Personal Safety Skills
PS:C1.10	Learn techniques for managing stress and conflict

Directions:

Follow the *All About You Catcher* directions on pages 42-43.

STRESS
Catcher

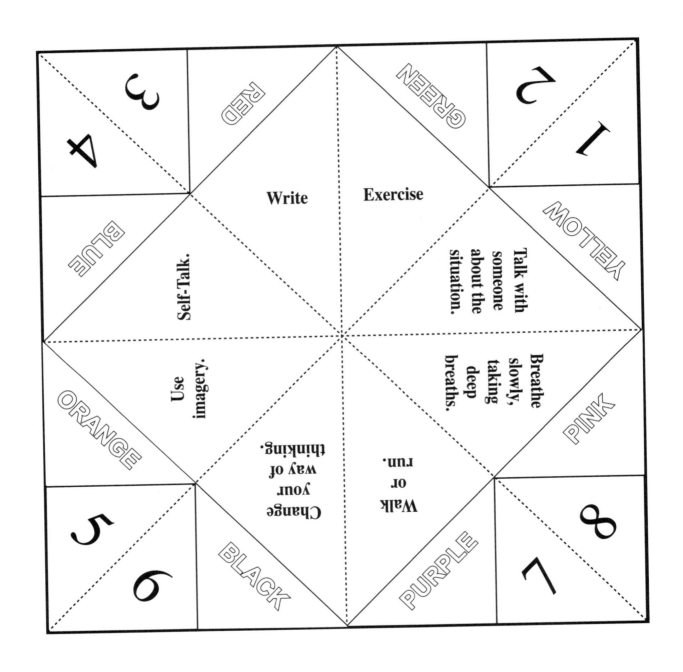

Ways To Amaze And Engage Middle School Students © 2009 Mar✳co Products, Inc. 1.800.448.2197

Circle Within A Circle

Purpose:

To allow students to practice listening skills

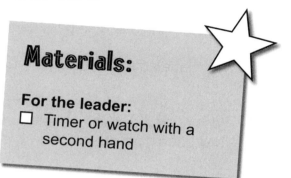

Materials:

For the leader:
☐ Timer or watch with a second hand

ASCA Standards:

PERSONAL/SOCIAL DEVELOPMENT	
Standard A: Students will acquire the knowledge, attitudes and interpersonal skills to help them understand and respect self and others.	
PS:A2	Acquire Interpersonal Skills
PS:A2.6	Use effective communications skills

Directions:

Have half of the students form a circle and face outward.

The other students form a circle around this inner circle. Each student in the outer circle should be facing a student in the inner circle.

Tell the students they are going to practice the good listening skills of *focusing* (looking at the person), *accepting* (nodding or saying "uh, uh" but not talking), then *giving feedback* (asking questions or commenting about what the speaker has said).

The students on the inside speak to the students on the outside about the subject the teacher/counselor has selected. The listeners will respond.

After one minute, the teacher/counselor will ask the person on the outside to talk about the same subject to the person on the inside. Once again, the students will have one minute to speak and respond.

When the allotted time has elapsed, the students on the outside take one step to the right. When they do, they will be facing a different student in the inner circle.

The teacher/counselor will select another topic. This time, the person in the outer circle will speak first to the person across from him/her. After one minute, the person in the inner circle will speak and the other student will respond. Then the people on the outside will take a step to the right, and will be facing someone new.

Continue until the students return to where they started.

The students may sit in chairs on the inside, facing outward and chairs on the outside facing inward. Each student on the outside moves to the next chair after each topic has been discussed.

Suggested discussion topics:

- Where would you like to visit?
- If a time machine could take you to any time and place in the past, when and where would you go?
- If you could live anywhere, where would you live?
- What would you like to do that you have never done?
- What do you look for in a friend?
- If you could change anything, what would it be?
- Talk about your best friend.
- Talk about your favorite movie.
- If someone called you right now, who would you want it to be?
- If you had to listen to the same song every day for the rest of your life, what would you want it to be?
- If you got to star in a movie, what movie would it be and what part would you play?
- If you could visit with anyone (living or dead) who would it be?
- What are your plans for the future?
- What is your favorite smell?
- What is your favorite thing to do?
- If you could go anywhere in the world, where would you go?
- If you were stranded on a desert island, what two things would you want to have with you?
- What would be your dream job?
- If you could see only one color for the rest of your life, what color would you want to see?
- What is your favorite time of the year?
- Whom would you like to meet and why?
- If you could choose a different name, what would it be?
- What is your favorite pet? Why?
- Talk about your family.
- If someone wrote a song about you, what would it be?
- What is the scariest thing that ever happened to you?

Ways To Amaze And Engage Middle School Students © 2009 Mar✷co Products, Inc. 1.800.448.2197

- What is the most joyful thing that ever happened to you?
- If you couldn't go to our school, what school would you like to attend?
- If you could eat lunch with someone famous, who would it be?
- Where is the best place that you ever have been?
- What is your favorite thing about school?
- If you could be on a TV show, what would it be? Who would you be?
- If you were given $1,000, what would you do with it?
- What is your idea of a perfect day?
- What is your dream?
- If you could live during any time period (past, present, future), what would you choose?
- If you were principal of this school, what would you do?
- If you had the power to change one thing in the world, what would you change?

Ways To Amaze And Engage Middle School Students © 2009 Mar*co Products, Inc. 1.800.448.2197

Class Quilt

Purpose:

To help students learn about their classmates

Materials:

For the leader:
- ☐ Large piece of bulletin board paper
- ☐ Stapler and staples
- ☐ Glue

For each student:
- ☐ 4" x 4" square of colored paper
- ☐ Pencil, pen, or marker

ASCA Standards:

PERSONAL/SOCIAL DEVELOPMENT	
Standard A: Students will acquire the knowledge, attitudes and interpersonal skills to help them understand and respect self and others.	
PS:A2	Acquire Interpersonal Skills
PS:A2.3	Recognize, accept, respect and appreciate individual differences

Directions:

Staple the bulletin board paper to the bulletin board.

Tell the students to fold the colored paper in half from corner to corner, then fold it in half using the other corners. This should create a 4-sided diamond shape.

Have the students write their names in the middle of the diamond and circle them.

Tell the students what to write in each area on their diamond-shaped paper (see *Variations* on page 53). (*Note:* This activity works especially well at the beginning of the school year.)

Starting in the center of the bulletin board, glue the diamond shapes together to look like a quilt.

Leave space at the edges of the bulletin board to serve as the quilt edges.

Ways To Amaze And Engage Middle School Students © 2009 Mar∗co Products, Inc. 1.800.448.2197

Across the top, write: "The Students in Room _____."

Variations:

- Have the students write four goals for this school year (Our Goals for this School Year).
- For a loss group, have the students write four *feeling words* to describe how they feel about their loss (Our Feelings About Loss).
- For an anger-management lesson, have the students write four healthy ways to handle anger (Healthy Ways to Handle Anger).
- Have the students write four reasons they will not use drugs (Reasons Not to Use Drugs).
- Have the students write four ways they get high on life (Ways to Get High on Life).

Display the quilt in the classroom.

Ways To Amaze And Engage Middle School Students © 2009 Mar∗co Products, Inc. 1.800.448.2197

Complaint Ball

Purpose:

To give students an opportunity to voice constructive criticism

Materials:

For the leader:
☐ Beach ball

ASCA Standards:

PERSONAL/SOCIAL DEVELOPMENT	
Standard A: Students will acquire the knowledge, attitudes and interpersonal skills to help them understand and respect self and others.	
PS:A2	Acquire Interpersonal Skills
PS:A2.2	Respect alternative points of view
PS:A2.6	Use effective communications skills

Directions:

The students stand in a circle.

Tell the students to raise their hand if they would like to complain about something. Someone will toss the beach ball to them.

A student who has the ball may complain about something. Demonstrate how to complain in a non-threatening environment. For example:

"I want to complain that we have to remain seated at our tables after we eat lunch. It would be nice to socialize with our other friends."

"I want to complain that we are one of the richest countries in the world, and everyone does not have health care."

Conclude the activity by:

- comparing complaints for similarities and differences
- asking if students believe something will or could be done about their complaint
- asking if students may have this same complaint in five or ten years

Concept/Vocabulary (Review Game)

Purpose:

To review vocabulary definitions

ASCA Standards:

These will depend on lesson being taught. The ASCA Standards below are for the examples given in this lesson.

Materials:

For the leader:
☐ Tagboard or construction paper cards marked with individual letters that spell the words of your definitions
or
Required *Alphabet Letters* printed from CD-Rom
☐ Marker

PERSONAL/SOCIAL DEVELOPMENT	
Standard A: Students will acquire the knowledge, attitudes and interpersonal skills to help them understand and respect self and others.	
PS:A2	Acquire Interpersonal Skills
PS:A2.7	Know that communication involves speaking, listening and nonverbal behavior

Directions:

Tell the students they are going to review vocabulary definitions. As you define a word, the students whose letters spell the answer to the definition silently go to the front of the room. Holding the letters, they form the vocabulary word. The leader will then review the concept of the word with the class. The students will then return to their seats.

Distribute the letters needed to spell the words. If possible, give each student one letter. Tell the students there will be no talking during this activity.

To review the terms: *Focus, Accept,* and *Give Feedback,* you'll need:

    1 – F
    1 – O
    2 – C

1 – U
1 – S
1 – A
3 – E
1 – P
1 – T
1 – G
1 – I
1 – V
1 – D
1 – B
1 – K

Read the first definition:

This means to look, turn, and/or lean toward the person who is speaking.

Students who have the letters in *FOCUS* go to the front of the room and spell their word for the class to see. Review the importance of this skill.

The students then sit down and the next definition is read:

This means to nod or say "uh, uh," while listening to someone talk.

Students with the letters in *ACCEPT* go to the front of the room and spell the word. Review this concept with the students.

The students then sit down and the next definition is read:

This means to stay on the subject, agree, disagree, ask questions, or comment.

Students with the letters in *GIVE FEEDBACK* go to the front of the room and form the words. Review this concept with the students.

Use this activity for any vocabulary words you want to review.

To review *aggressive*, *passive*, and *assertive*, you'll need:

1 – A
2 – G
1 – R
2 – E
2 – S
1 – I

Ways To Amaze And Engage Middle School Students © 2009 Mar✳co Products, Inc. 1.800.448.2197

1 – V
1 – P
1 – T

Give the first definition:

To speak with confidence and assurance, without blaming, to let others know how you feel.

Students with the letters in *ASSERTIVE* come to the front of the room and spell the word. Discuss the benefits of being assertive.

The students then sit down and the next definition is read:

Being offensive to others and/or forceful.

Students with the letters in *AGGRESSIVE* come to the front of the room and spell the word. Discuss the consequences of aggressive behavior.

The students then sit down and the last definition is read:

Taking no action, not reacting visibly to something. Being submissive.

Students with the letters in *PASSIVE* spell that word. Discuss when passive behavior can be good and not so good.

Ways To Amaze And Engage Middle School Students © 2009 Mar∗co Products, Inc. 1.800.448.2197

Cross The Line

Purpose:

To help students get to know each other and identify examples of *relational aggression*

Materials:

None required

ASCA Standards:

PERSONAL/SOCIAL DEVELOPMENT	
Standard A: Students will acquire the knowledge, attitudes and interpersonal skills to help them understand and respect self and others.	
PS:A1	Acquire Self-Knowledge
PS:A1.6	Distinguish between appropriate and inappropriate behavior
Standard C: Students will understand safety and survival skills.	
PS:C1	Acquire Personal Safety Skills
PS:C1.4	Demonstrate the ability to set boundaries, rights and personal privacy
PS:C1.11	Learn coping skills for managing life events

Directions:

This activity can be used when students are getting to know each other or relational aggression is being taught. Students must be able to answer with "yes" or "no."

The students stand in a straight line around the room. Say that you'll read a series of statements. Students who can answer "yes" to a statement take one step forward. After everyone who qualifies has moved forward, the students move back before the next statement is read.

Getting To Know You Statements:

- I'm the oldest in my family.
- I'm the youngest in my family.
- I have more than two siblings.
- I'm an only child.
- Math is my favorite subject.

☆ 58 ☆

- I like to write.
- I love to read.
- I enjoy coming to school.
- I can trust my best friend.
- I think I know what I want to be when I grow up.
- Evening is my favorite part of the day.
- Summer is my favorite season.
- I would like to travel outside of the U.S.A. some day.
- I like to play videogames.
- If I had $500, I would give some of it to charity.
- I like to watch movies.
- I play a sport.
- I'm in a club at school.
- I take/have taken piano lessons.
- I take/have taken gymnastics.
- My grandparents live in the town where I live.

To see how observant students were, have them name those who answered "yes" for specified questions.

The activity below deals with relational aggression. Ask the students to move forward if they can answer "yes."

- Has anyone ever rolled his/her eyes at you?
- Have you ever rolled your eyes at someone?
- Has anyone ever ignored you?
- Have you ever ignored someone?
- Have you ever been excluded from something?
- Have you ever excluded anyone?
- Have you ever been the subject of a rumor?
- Have you ever repeated or started a rumor?
- Has anyone ever made fun of you?
- Have you ever made fun of anyone?
- Has anyone ever gossiped about you?
- Have you ever gossiped about anyone?
- Has anyone ever tricked you into saying or writing negative things about someone you didn't know was listening or watching?
- Have you ever tricked someone into saying or writing something negative about someone who was secretly watching or listening?
- Has anyone ever been nice to you to your face, then talked negatively about you behind your back?
- Have you ever been nice to someone, then talked negatively about him/her behind his/her back?

- Has anyone ever cyber-bullied you?
- Have you ever cyber-bullied anyone?

Point out that these bullying behaviors hurt others. Students who are doing these things should stop. Students to whom these things are being done must tell an adult. It's never OK to intentionally hurt another person. Nor is it OK for another person to intentionally hurt you.

Ways To Amaze And Engage Middle School Students © 2009 Mar∗co Products, Inc. 1.800.448.2197

Deep Breathing

Purpose:

To teach a relaxation technique

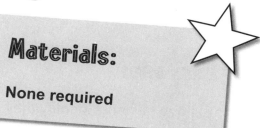

Materials:

None required

ASCA Standards:

PERSONAL/SOCIAL DEVELOPMENT	
Standard C: Students will understand safety and survival skills.	
PS:C1	Acquire Personal Safety Skills
PS:C1.10	Learn techniques for managing stress and conflict

Directions:

Tell the students to picture drawing a box when they practice deep breathing:

1. In your mind, draw a line going down. Breathe in, counting *1, 2, 3, 4.*
2. Draw a line going across. Hold your breath, counting *1, 2, 3, 4.*
3. Draw a line going up. Breathe out, counting *1, 2, 3, 4.*
4. Draw a line across to close the box. Relax, counting *1, 2, 3, 4.*

Breathe deeply and slowly.

Ways To Amaze And Engage Middle School Students © 2009 Mar*co Products, Inc. 1.800.448.2197

Dream Board

Purpose:

To have students identify their dreams and goals

ASCA Standards:

ACADEMIC DEVELOPMENT	
Standard B: Students will complete school with the academic preparation essential to choose from a wide range of substantial post- secondary options, including college.	
A:B2	Plan To Achieve Goals
A:B2.4	Apply knowledge of aptitudes and interests to goal setting

Directions:

Discuss the difference between *goals* and *dreams*. A *goal* is realistic and attainable. A *dream* is not necessarily realistic or attainable.

Discuss *short-term goals* and *long-term goals*. Ask for examples of each type of goal. Short-term goals may include getting on the honor roll, making a sports team, getting a job, etc. Long-term goals may include working in a specific career, attending a certain college, living in a certain area, traveling, writing a book, etc. Have the students brainstorm some of the short- and long-term goals they hope to achieve. Remind them that goals change.

Tell the students they are going to create their Dream Board, which should consist of things they hope to accomplish. Students may decorate their Dream Board by cutting pictures or words from the magazines and/or writing things that pertain to their dreams and goals.

Tell the students to take their completed Dream Boards home and look at them every day. Make it clear that the Dream Boards are works in progress and that students may change or add to them.

Ways To Amaze And Engage Middle School Students © 2009 Mar∗co Products, Inc. 1.800.448.2197

Everybody Has A Story

Purpose:

To help students learn more about classmates

Materials:

For the leader:
- ☐ Container

For each student:
- ☐ 5 index cards or 5 small pieces of paper
- ☐ Pencil

ASCA Standards:

PERSONAL/SOCIAL DEVELOPMENT	
Standard A: Students will acquire the knowledge, attitudes and interpersonal skills to help them understand and respect self and others.	
PS:A1	Acquire Self-Knowledge
PS:A1.1	Develop positive attitudes toward self as a unique and worthy person
PS:A2	Acquire Interpersonal Skills
PS:A2.3	Recognize, accept, respect and appreciate individual differences

Directions:

On each card or piece of paper, ask the students to write an open-ended question or statement that can be directed to anyone. Give examples like:

- If you could visit anywhere in the world, where would you go?
- Tell us about your family.
- Tell us about your best friend.
- When was the last time you laughed so hard that you cried?
- If someone called you right now, who would you want it to be?

Place the completed cards in the container.

Students take turns drawing five cards.

Ask each student to read and answer the question on each of the five cards drawn. A student who has answered the questions may choose the next person to repeat the activity.

This activity can be completed in one class period. It's a good activity for the end of a lesson. If you will be in a classroom for a few sessions and have time, you may want to have five different students participate in this activity at the end of each lesson. Make sure that by the time your lessons are completed, every student has had a turn.

"Go-To" Person

Purpose:

To have students identify an adult they can "go to" for advice

Materials:

For each student:
- ☐ Index card
- ☐ Pen or pencil

ASCA Standards:

PERSONAL/SOCIAL DEVELOPMENT	
Standard C: Students will understand safety and survival skills.	
PS:C1	Acquire Personal Safety Skills
PS:C1.6	Identify resource people in the school and community, and know how to seek their help

Directions:

Talk to the students about the importance of having a "go-to" person—an adult they can go to if they are being bullied or having other problems.

Emphasize that every student should have at least one person in the school in whom he/she can confide.

Ask what qualities in an adult would make students feel comfortable about reporting that someone is not treating them well. Some examples are: being trustworthy, open-minded, approachable, a good listener, and someone who would handle the situation. Let the students know that a go-to person might be an administrator or counselor, but could be any adult staff member. Emphasize that this person should be someone with whom the student can talk comfortably.

Tell the students to write on the index card the name of a person in the school to whom he/she would report being treated badly.

Make sure everyone has written a name of an adult in the school.

You may want to ask if anyone would like to share the name of his/her "go-to" person.

Optional: Post the index cards on the bulletin board for everyone to see.

Ways To Amaze And Engage Middle School Students © 2009 Mar✶co Products, Inc. 1.800.448.2197

Identifying Character Traits

Purpose:

To have students identify and define specific character traits

Materials:

For the leader:
- ☐ Board or chart paper and marker
- ☐ Piece of 8 ½" x 11" tagboard for each trait listed
or
Medium-weight paper for printing the character-trait cards (included on CD-Rom)

ASCA Standards:

PERSONAL/SOCIAL DEVELOPMENT	
Standard A: Students will acquire the knowledge, attitudes and interpersonal skills to help them understand and respect self and others.	
PS:A1	Acquire Self-Knowledge
PS:A1.2	Identify values, attitudes and beliefs
PS:A2	Acquire Interpersonal Skills
PS:A2.6	Use effective communications skills

Directions:

Write each character trait listed below and on page 67 on a piece of tagboard or print the traits from the CD. Put the completed tagboards face down in a pile.

Begin the lesson by writing the following character traits on the board or chart paper:

Courage	Gratitude	Respect
Responsibility	Cooperation	Honesty
Fairness	Caring	Trustworthiness
Humility	Loyalty	Generosity

Self-confidence   Consideration   Friendliness
Helpfulness   Ambition   Determination
Thoughtfulness

Discuss the meaning of each word, having the students tell when they've seen others display these traits.

Choose one student at a time to come to the front of the room.

Hold a trait card above the student's head. The rest of the class can see the word, but he/she can't.

The student may ask three yes/no questions about the trait.

After three questions have been answered, the student asks a fourth question that includes his/her guess about what the trait is.

For example: The word is *honest*.

The student asks:

- Does the word describe someone who helps others? (no)
- Does our teacher have this trait? (yes)
- Does the word describe someone who tells the truth? (yes)
- Is the word *honest*? (yes)

Continue until everyone who wants a turn gets one. Some words may be repeated.

Alternative:

Use paper headbands labeled with the traits.

Imagery

Purpose:

To teach relaxation techniques

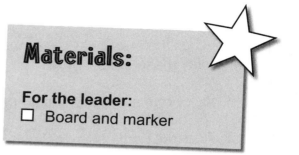

Materials:

For the leader:
☐ Board and marker

ASCA Standards:

PERSONAL/SOCIAL DEVELOPMENT	
Standard C: Students will understand safety and survival skills.	
PS:C1	Acquire Personal Safety Skills
PS:C1.10	Learn techniques for managing stress and conflict

Directions:

Tell the students that imagery can help them relax and that this lesson will take them through guided imagery.

Say:

- Get comfortable in your chairs with your feet on the ground.
- Close your eyes.
- You're going to go up in a very safe hot-air balloon.
- You can:
    - stay in this room
    - soar to your favorite place
    - fly to visit a friend or relative
- Make your choice.
- Now get into the hot-air balloon and go.
- The hot-air balloon lands. Get out of the basket and visit the place of your choice.

Give the students one or two minutes to be in that place. Then say:

- It's time to get back into the hot-air balloon and return to this room.
- When you return, you may open your eyes.

Discuss the following questions:

- Who chose to stay in this room?
- Who went to a favorite place? Where? Why?
- Who visited a friend or relative? Who? Why?

Tell the students that when they feel stressed, they can take themselves someplace in their mind. This will help them relax.

Ask what the students picture to help them relax. List their responses on the board.

Examples are:

- Fire in a fireplace
- Warm, soft blankets
- Listening to the ocean
- Walking in the woods
- Looking at mountains
- Lying in a bed of cotton
- Being in the clouds
- Watching the rain

Koosh® Ball Name Game

Purpose:

To have students learn classmates' names and participate in a cooperative group activity

Materials:

For the leader:
☐ 3–5 Koosh balls

ASCA Standards:

PERSONAL/SOCIAL DEVELOPMENT	
Standard A: Students will acquire the knowledge, attitudes and interpersonal skills to help them understand and respect self and others.	
PS:A1	Acquire Self-Knowledge
PS:A1.9	Demonstrate cooperative behavior in groups
PS:A2	Acquire Interpersonal Skills
PS:A2.7	Know that communication involves speaking, listening and nonverbal behavior

Directions:

The students stand in a circle.

Explain that the purpose of the game is for each student to learn another student's name by repeating it several times. When a student throws a ball, he/she will call out the name of the person to whom the ball is thrown. The student catching the ball will then call out another student's name and throw the ball to him/her.

Assign each student another student to whom he/she will throw the ball. The leader will also choose a student to begin each round and a student to end each round by throwing the ball back to the leader. Begin the game with a practice round. The leader will throw one ball to the chosen student, calling out the student's name. The student catching the ball will then call out his/her assigned student's name and throw the ball to that person. The process will be repeated until the ball is returned to the leader.

Ways To Amaze And Engage Middle School Students © 2009 Mar✶co Products, Inc. 1.800.448.2197

Once the leader is satisfied that the students understand how he game is played, several balls should be introduced. The process is the same except that instead of having only one ball being used, the leader will throw several balls, one after the other, so that the balls are in play at the same time. The game continues in this manner with the students always catching the ball when their name is called and throwing it to the same person each time while calling out that person's name.

(*Note:* This activity is appropriate for small groups and classrooms.)

Letter To Self

Purpose:

To have students set goals for the new school year

Materials:

For each student:
- ☐ Paper
- ☐ Envelope
- ☐ Pen or pencil

ASCA Standards:

PERSONAL/SOCIAL DEVELOPMENT	
Standard A: Students will acquire the knowledge, attitudes and interpersonal skills to help them understand and respect self and others.	
PS:A1	Acquire Self-Knowledge
PS:A1.3	Learn the goal-setting process
Standard B: Students will make decisions, set goals and take necessary action to achieve goals.	
PS:B1	Self-Knowledge Application
PS:B1.12	Develop an action plan to set and achieve realistic goals

Directions:

Discuss students' hopes and goals for the new school year. At the end of the discussion, each student writes a letter to him/herself and places it in a sealed envelope addressed with his/her name. The letter should describe what the student hopes to accomplish by the end of the school year.

Keep the collected letters in safe place.

At the end of the school year, return the letters. Encourage the students to write about their accomplishments this school year and whether they met their goals.

If not, why not? If so, what does that feel like? Did they have to adjust or change any goals? What has changed and what has not?

After the students have finished, ask them to share what they have written.

Alternative:

Students entering middle school or high school write to themselves about what they hope to accomplish in the next three or four years. They may describe friends, grades, what they hope will happen, etc. At the end of their last year, distribute the letters to the students who wrote them. Students who wish to do so may share their letters with the class/group.

Variation:

Parents/guardians write a letter to their children when they begin middle school or high school and seal the envelope. At the end of middle school or before graduation, the students read what their parents/guardians wrote to them three or four years earlier.

Ways To Amaze And Engage Middle School Students © 2009 Mar*co Products, Inc. 1.800.448.2197

Line Drill

Purpose:

To have students work together in a group

Materials:

None required

ASCA Standards:

PERSONAL/SOCIAL DEVELOPMENT	
Standard A: Students will acquire the knowledge, attitudes and interpersonal skills to help them understand and respect self and others.	
PS:A1	Acquire Self-Knowledge
PS:A1.9	Demonstrate cooperative behavior in groups
Standard C: Students will understand safety and survival skills.	
PS:C1	Acquire Personal Safety Skills
PS:C1.11	Learn coping skills for managing life events

Directions:

Divide the students into two or four groups.

Each group forms a straight line, one student behind the other.

The first person in line turns to the person behind him/her and gives an answer to a topic selected by the leader. Then the first person goes to the back of the line.

The person who is now first in line turns to the person behind him/her and, using the same topic, repeats the procedure. No answer may be repeated.

The game continues until everyone has had a turn and the person who was originally in the front of the line is again in that position.

The first team to complete the activity sits down and wins.

Ways To Amaze And Engage Middle School Students © 2009 Mar∗co Products, Inc. 1.800.448.2197

Suggested topics are:

- healthy ways to handle anger
- reasons not to use drugs
- ways to get high on life (not using drugs or alcohol)
- complimenting the person behind you
- good study habits
- healthy ways to relieve stress

Use this game to review any topic.

Ways To Amaze And Engage Middle School Students © 2009 Mar★co Products, Inc. 1.800.448.2197

Map Of The School

Purpose:

To have students identify where bullying occurs in school

Materials:

For the leader:
- [ ] Board and marker

For each student:
- [ ] Copy of map of school
- [ ] Pencil

ASCA Standards:

Standard C: Students will understand safety and survival skills.	
PS:C1	Acquire Personal Safety Skills
PS:C1.5	Differentiate between situations requiring peer support and situations requiring adult professional help

Directions:

Use this activity in all or a number of classes.

On a map of the school, students mark the three places where bullying occurs most often.

Ask what places each student marked. Tally the results on the board.

Look at the top three places the students chose. Compare them with answers from students in other classes.

Share the results with staff and administrators, so they can make sure those areas are supervised.

Additional Activity:

Divide the students into groups. Using the tally, have each group write bullying-prevention plans for the school. Share their results with the class.

Match Puzzle Piece (Review Game)

Purpose:

To review concepts or vocabulary

ASCA Standards:

The applicable ASCA Standards would depend on the topic to be reviewed

Materials:

For the leader:
- ☐ Tagboard
  or
  Copies of selected *Shapes* (pages 78-80 or CD-Rom)
- ☐ Scissors
- ☐ Marker or pen

Directions:

A good way to review a lesson is to select a *Shape* or choose one of your own. Reproduce or priint enough shapes for half of the group. Cut out the shapes, then cut each shape in half like puzzle pieces, so they fit together perfectly. Cut each shape differently. On one half of each shape, write a word learned in a previous lesson. On the second half of each shape, write the definition.

Give each student half of a shape.

When everyone has found his/her match, the students fit their shapes together. Each shape should be read aloud to reinforce the previous lesson.

(*Note:* This is particularly suitable during a holiday season. On Valentine's Day, for example, cut heart shapes in half. Mix them up and pass them out to students. Students pair up with the person who has the other half of their heart.)

Other shapes you can use are:

- January—snowflake
- February—heart
- March—shamrock
- April/May—flower
- September—book
- October—pumpkin
- November—turkey
- December—star
- Any time—puzzle piece

SHAPES

SHAPES

SHAPES

Name Acrostic

Purpose:

To enhance students' self-esteem

Materials:

For each student:
- ☐ Piece of 11½" x 18" paper
- ☐ Markers
- ☐ Optional: Thesaurus

ASCA Standards:

PERSONAL/SOCIAL DEVELOPMENT	
Standard A: Students will acquire the knowledge, attitudes and interpersonal skills to help them understand and respect self and others.	
PS:A1	Acquire Self-Knowledge
PS:A1.9	Demonstrate cooperative behavior in groups
PS:A1.10	Identify personal strengths and assets

Directions:

Students write their first name vertically on the left side of the paper, evenly spacing the letters below one another.

Each student should write a positive word or phrase that describes him/herself and begins with a letter in his/her name. It may be helpful to use a thesaurus for this activity.

Variation:

Divide the students into groups of four. Tell each group member to use a different-color marker. Students should switch papers with other group members. Each student will write something positive about another group member, for each of the letters in that person's name.

When the activity is completed, four words should be written for each letter in each student's name.

Have each person share his/her name acrostic with the class. Display the papers in the classroom.

Open-Ended Statements

Purpose:

To have students learn more about each other

Materials:

For the leader:
☐ *Open-Ended Statements* (pages 83-85 or CD-Rom)
☐ Scissors
☐ Container

ASCA Standards:

PERSONAL/SOCIAL DEVELOPMENT	
Standard A: Students will acquire the knowledge, attitudes and interpersonal skills to help them understand and respect self and others.	
PS:A2	Acquire Interpersonal Skills
PS:A2.2	Respect alternative points of view
PS:A2.6	Use effective communications skills

Directions:

Open-ended statements make good energizers, are a good way for students to learn more about each other and for the facilitator to learn more about the students, and are good to use if time permits at the end of the period.

Reproduce or print the *Open-Ended Statements*, cut them apart, and place them in the container.

Have a student draw one statement from the container, complete the statement, and place it back in the container. Continue until each student has had an opportunity to complete an *Open-Ended Statement.*

Ask each student to state one thing he/she learned about another student during this activity. (*Note:* Jot down any answers that may need further investigation.)

Ways To Amaze And Engage Middle School Students © 2009 Mar*co Products, Inc. 1.800.448.2197

OPEN-ENDED STATEMENTS

If I could visit anywhere, it would be…

If I could go back in time, I'd want to live…

I'd like to visit…

I hope to some day…

The best thing about my best friend is…

I'd like to complain about…

It just takes too long to…

My favorite movie is…

My favorite song/musical group is…

If I could get a call from anyone, I'd want it to be…

The movie I'd want to star in is…

If I could eat lunch with anyone in the world,
I'd choose…

My future plans are…

My favorite thing to do is…

One thing that angered me recently…

One thing that made me happy recently…

My all-time favorite teacher is…

If I had $1,000, I'd…

My dream is…

My idea of a perfect day is…

My favorite month is…

The best vacation I ever had…

If I were principal of this school, I'd…

I had and lost…

If a book was written about me, the title would be…

One thing I hope to accomplish in my life is…

Other kids…

If I could choose a different name, I'd choose…

Tell about your pets. If you don't have one, tell about a pet you wish you had.

A risk I took was…

Would you want to work for yourself if you were the boss? Why or why not?

If one of your teachers could be your older brother or sister, whom would you choose?

The best advice I ever received was…

Ways To Amaze And Engage Middle School Students © 2009 Mar∗co Products, Inc. 1.800.448.2197

Paper Chain

Purpose:

To have students get to know and appreciate others

Materials:

For the leader:
- ☐ Colored paper
- ☐ Scissors
- ☐ Stapler and staples or glue

For each student:
- ☐ Pencil or marker

ASCA Standards:

PERSONAL/SOCIAL DEVELOPMENT	
Standard A: Students will acquire the knowledge, attitudes and interpersonal skills to help them understand and respect self and others.	
PS:A1	Acquire Self-Knowledge
PS:A1.1	Develop positive attitudes toward self as a unique and worthy person
PS:A2	Acquire Interpersonal Skills
PS:A2.3	Recognize, accept, respect and appreciate individual differences

Directions:

Cut colored paper into 3″ x 1″ strips. Each student should have four strips.

Tell the students to write, on each strip of paper, their names and something about the chosen topic (see suggested topics below).

- **Our Goals for This School Year**: Have the students write four of their goals for this school year.
- **Our Feelings About Loss**: For a loss group, have the students write four *feeling words* to describe how they feel about their loss.
- **Healthy Ways to Handle Anger**: For an anger-management lesson, have the students write four healthy ways to handle anger.
- **Reasons Not to Use Drugs**: Have the students write four reasons they won't use drugs.

Once the students have finished writing, glue or staple the strips together to make a chain. Hang the chain in the classroom.

Ways To Amaze And Engage Middle School Students © 2009 Mar∗co Products, Inc. 1.800.448.2197

Paper Plate Saucers

Purpose:

To have students become better acquainted

Materials:

For each student:
☐ Paper plate
☐ Pen or pencil

ASCA Standards:

PERSONAL/SOCIAL DEVELOPMENT	
Standard A: Students will acquire the knowledge, attitudes and interpersonal skills to help them understand and respect self and others.	
PS:A2	Acquire Interpersonal Skills
PS:A2.3	Recognize, accept, respect and appreciate individual differences

Directions:

The students should not write their name on the paper plate. They should write numbers from *1* to *5,* leaving room between each number to answer the following questions:

- If someone called you right now, who would you want it to be?
- What's your favorite thing to do?
- Whom do you admire?
- What's a pet peeve of yours?
- What's the best thing that could happen to you?

When the students have answered the questions, they stand and throw the saucers (paper plates) to each other. They keep picking up the saucers and throwing them to different people until the leader tells them to stop. They then take one saucer and sit down. The students take turns reading aloud the answers on those saucers and trying to guess who wrote them.

Variation:

On a rainy day, students write their answers on cut-out *Raindrops* (page 88 or CD-Rom), then throw the raindrops into the air, watch them fall, and pick up different ones each time. When the leader tells them to stop, each student picks up a raindrop. The students take turns reading aloud the answers on those raindrops and trying to guess who wrote them.

RAINDROPS

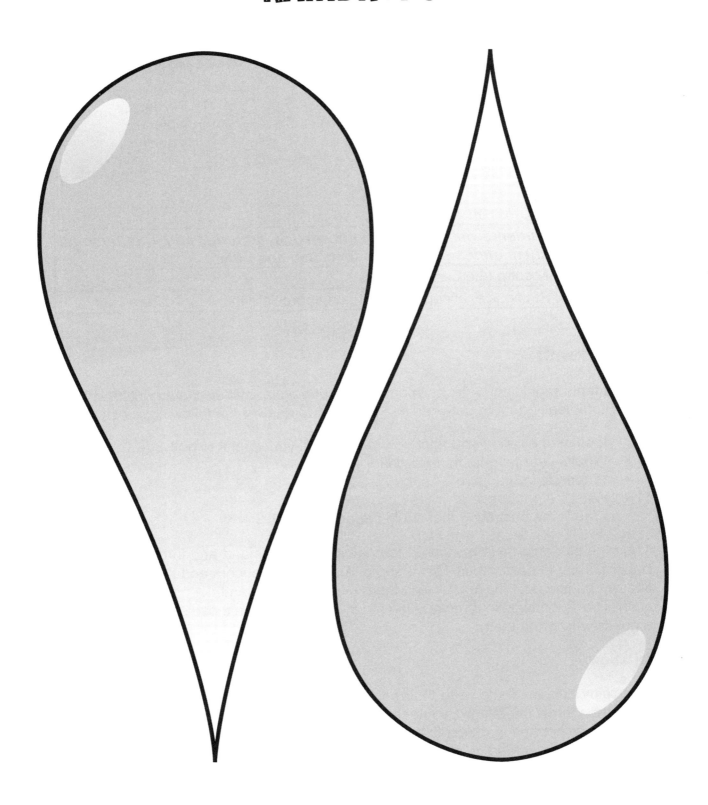

People Search

Purpose:

To have students become better acquainted

Materials:

For each student:
- [ ] *People Search* (page 90 or CD-Rom) or *Who Is Just Like Me?* (page 91 or CD-Rom)
- [ ] Pen or pencil

ASCA Standards:

PERSONAL/SOCIAL DEVELOPMENT	
Standard A: Students will acquire the knowledge, attitudes and interpersonal skills to help them understand and respect self and others.	
PS:A2	Acquire Interpersonal Skills
PS:A2.3	Recognize, accept, respect and appreciate individual differences

Directions:

This is a good way for students to get to know one another. It's especially helpful when students are together for the first time, like at the beginning of the school year.

People Search is similar to a Bingo board. Students initial a box whose question pertains to them. For *Who Is Just Like Me?*, students first answer questions about themselves, then look for two other people in the room whose answers match theirs.

When the students have completed an activity sheet and returned to their seats, have them share their answers with the class/group.

PEOPLE SEARCH

Directions: Move around the room looking for people whose experience or habits pertain to what's written in each box. When you find a person, have him/her initial the box. A student may initial only one box on each person's *People Search*. When all the boxes on your paper have been initialed, sit down. If a box can't be initialed by anyone in the class, leave the box blank.

Has blue eyes	Is left-handed	Has visited another country	Plays the piano	Is in the band
Writes poetry	Is an only child	Is new to our school this year	Has won an award	Likes math best
Has gotten all A's on his/her report card	Has helped someone out this week	Likes yellow best	Can speak another language	Has an internet social networking page
Has a brother or sister in our school	Plays basketball	Has a best friend who attends another school	Sings well	Has met someone famous

Ways To Amaze And Engage Middle School Students © 2009 Mar*co Products, Inc. 1.800.448.2197

WHO IS JUST LIKE ME?

Directions: Answer each question on the worksheet. Find two other people who have the same answer you do. Have them initial your paper. When all your answers have been initialed by two students, sit down. If you can't find two people with the same answer as yours, leave the box blank.

TOPIC	YOUR ANSWERS	INITIALS	INITIALS
Favorite color			
Birthday month			
Favorite TV show			
Favorite flavor of ice cream			
State in which you were born			
Birth order (oldest, middle, youngest, only)			
Favorite subject			
Color of eyes			
Favorite song			
Favorite snack			
Favorite book			
Number of siblings			
Earned an award for			
Favorite movie			

☆ 91 ☆

Person Of The Year

Purpose:

To have students set goals

Materials:

For each student:
- ☐ Large piece of paper or *Person Of The Year* (page 93 or CD-Rom)
- ☐ Pen or pencil
- ☐ Markers

ASCA Standards:

PERSONAL/SOCIAL DEVELOPMENT	
Standard B: Students will make decisions, set goals and take necessary action to achieve goals.	
PS:B1	Self-Knowledge Application
PS:B1.12	Develop an action plan to set and achieve realistic goals

Directions:

If using blank paper, have the students fold it in half like a magazine cover.

Tell each student to imagine being selected *Person Of The Year.* Allow the students to choose their own year or assign them all the same year.

Each student puts a picture of him/herself in the bottom box on the cover. He/she may draw the picture or use a photo.

On the cover, each student should write his/her name in the banner. In the middle box, the student should write why he/she was selected *Person Of The Year.* If the year is in the future, have the students think about what goals they hope to accomplish and why those accomplishments led to this prestigious award. List these accomplishments on the cover.

Students share completed magazine covers with the group/class. Display the pictures in the classroom.

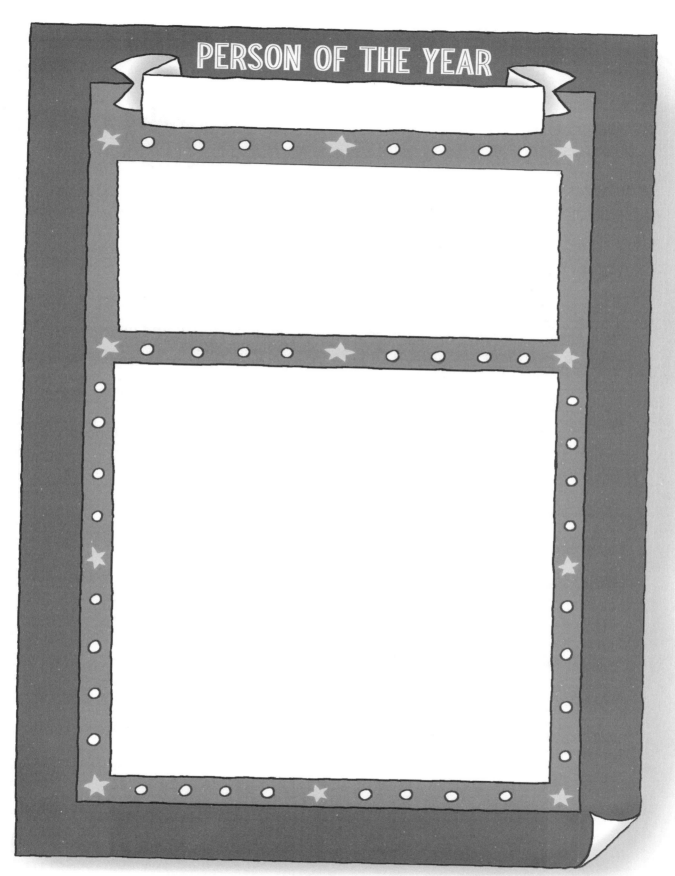

Ways To Amaze And Engage Middle School Students © 2009 Mar*co Products, Inc. 1.800.448.2197

Positive Bouncing Ball

Purpose:

To help students develop a positive attitude toward themselves and others

Materials:

For the leader:
☐ Ball that bounces

ASCA Standards:

PERSONAL/SOCIAL DEVELOPMENT	
Standard A: Students will acquire the knowledge, attitudes and interpersonal skills to help them understand and respect self and others.	
PS:A1	Acquire Self-Knowledge
PS:A1.1	Develop positive attitudes toward self as a unique and worthy person
PS:A2	Acquire Interpersonal Skills
PS:A2.3	Recognize, accept, respect and appreciate individual differences

Directions:

Students stand in a circle.

Explain that the ball will be bounced from person to person. A student who gets the ball bounces it to another person and says two positive things about him/her.

The person who catches the ball must repeat the two positive things, then bounce the ball to another person and say two positive things about him/her.

No person may receive the ball more than once.

Continue until everyone has heard two positive messages about him/herself and given two positive messages to another person.

Ways To Amaze And Engage Middle School Students © 2009 Mar∗co Products, Inc. 1.800.448.2197

Positive Messages

Purpose:

To have students recognize, accept, respect, and appreciate the individuality of others

Materials:

For the leader:
- ☐ Masking tape

For each student:
- ☐ Paper plate
- ☐ Marker

ASCA Standards:

PERSONAL/SOCIAL DEVELOPMENT	
Standard A: Students will acquire the knowledge, attitudes and interpersonal skills to help them understand and respect self and others.	
PS:A2	Acquire Interpersonal Skills
PS:A2.3	Recognize, accept, respect and appreciate individual differences

Directions:

Students write their name in the middle of the paper plate.

Tape each student's paper plate to his/her back.

Students walk around the room and write something positive on each person's paper plate. Before beginning, ask for examples of what someone may write. (*Note:* When discussing giving positive messages, encourage students to write what they like about the person. Discourage writing about clothes, hair, shoes, or appearance.)

After each student has written a positive message to everyone and received one from everyone, the students sit down, remove their paper plates, and read what others wrote about them.

Variation 1:

Students write their name in the middle of an 11″ x 16″ paper. When the teacher/counselor says to begin, the students pass their paper to the person behind them. Once they get another person's paper, they write something positive about him/her.

Ways To Amaze And Engage Middle School Students © 2009 Mar✶co Products, Inc. 1.800.448.2197

Then each student passes that paper to the person behind him/her. Continue until everyone has written on all the papers and each paper ends up with its owner. Give the students time to read the positive messages others wrote about them.

If you are presenting this activity to a small group, reproduce *Positive Messages For* _____ (page 97 or CD-Rom) and use it for the previous activity.

Variation 2:

Give each student one index card for every other student in the class or group. Feature each student in turn. Everyone in the class writes and signs a positive note to the featured student. When everyone has finished writing, the students read their notes aloud and give them to the person about whom they're written. Continue until each student has been featured. This is especially effective in small groups.

Ways To Amaze And Engage Middle School Students © 2009 Mar✳co Products, Inc. 1.800.448.2197

POSITIVE MESSAGES FOR

Friendly · helpful · Nice · Great · Smart · #1 · generous · Happy · #1 · sweet · Outgoing · genuine · GOOD

Power Beads

Purpose:

To have students recognize character traits and identify reasons to be drug-free

Materials:

For each student:
- ☐ 8 different-colored beads (red, clear, orange, green, white, pink, yellow, blue)
- ☐ Scissors
- ☐ Twine or elastic thread
- ☐ Optional: *Power Beads* (page 99 or CD-Rom)

ASCA Standards:

PERSONAL/SOCIAL DEVELOPMENT	
Standard A: Students will acquire the knowledge, attitudes and interpersonal skills to help them understand and respect self and others.	
PS:A1	Acquire Self-Knowledge
PS:A1.10	Identify personal strengths and assets
Standard B: Students will make decisions, set goals and take necessary action to achieve goals.	
PS:B1	Self-Knowledge Application
PS:B1.4	Develop effective coping skills for dealing with problems
Standard C: Students will understand safety and survival skills.	
PS:C1	Acquire Personal Safety Skills
PS:C1.11	Learn coping skills for managing life events

Directions:

When presenting a character-education or drug abuse-prevention lesson, have the students make bracelets. Each bead stands for a character trait or for a reason to be drug- free.

Each student cuts off a piece of twine or elastic thread the size of his/her wrist plus enough extra to make a knot.

Students string their beads according to the *Power Beads* color chart, tie off the ends, and wear the bracelet. Or the students assign traits to colors or write their own reasons to stay drug-free.

Ways To Amaze And Engage Middle School Students © 2009 Mar*co Products, Inc. 1.800.448.2197

POWER BEADS

Each bead represents a reason to stay drug-free.

Red   LOVE for family, friends, yourself
Clear   CLEAR mind, free of drugs
Orange   ENERGY, staying active
Green   RESPECT for yourself and others
White   CONTENTMENT, peace of mind
Pink   HEALTH, a body free of drugs and alcohol
Yellow   HAPPINESS, laughter
Blue   DREAMS, reach for yours

POWER BEADS

Each bead represents a positive character trait.

Red   COURAGE
Clear   TRUSTWORTHINESS
Orange   RESPONSIBILITY
Green   HELPFULNESS
White   HONESTY
Pink   FRIENDLINESS
Yellow   KINDNESS
Blue   DEPENDABILITY

Ways To Amaze And Engage Middle School Students © 2009 Mar*co Products, Inc. 1.800.448.2197

Right Brain/Left Brain

Purpose:

To teach students the difference between using his/her right brain and left brain and the qualities each possesses

Materials:

For each group recorder:
- ☐ Pen or pencil
- ☐ Paper

ASCA Standards:

ACADEMIC DEVELOPMENT	
Standard A: Students will acquire the attitudes, knowledge and skills that contribute to effective learning in school and across the life span.	
A:A3	Achieve School Success
A:A3.2	Demonstrate the ability to work independently, as well as the ability to work cooperatively with other students
Standard B: Students will complete school with the academic preparation essential to choose from a wide range of substantial post- secondary options, including college.	
A:B1	Improve Learning
A:B1.3	Apply the study skills necessary for academic success at each level

Directions:

Explain that you're going to explore the right brain/left brain concept.

Students fold their hands. Tell them it's said that if the left thumb is below the right thumb, they use their left brain more. If the right thumb is below the left thumb, they use their right brain more.

Students cross their arms. Tell them that if the right arm is above the left arm, they use their left brain more. If the left arm is above the right arm, they use their right brain more.

Have right-brained students go to one area of the room and left-brained students go to another.

Students who were right- or left-brained on one activity and the opposite on the other stand in the middle of the room.

Each group selects a recorder and thinks of qualities group members share. The recorder makes notes. Do group members like structured or unstructured situations? Do they like to play it safe or take risks? Are they imaginative or analytical? Compare the lists.

Tell the students that a left-brained student can be a perfectionist and is likely to be:

- analytical
- verbal
- detail-oriented
- cautious
- logical
- reasonable
- trustworthy
- practical

A right-brained student is apt to take risks, dislike schedules or structure, and is likely to be:

- visual
- spatially oriented
- emotional
- artistic
- spontaneous
- imaginative

Ask the students if their responses reflect these qualities.

Say that it's good to have left- and right-brained students work together in groups. Ask if the students agree or disagree with this statement and why.

Ask students how they can benefit from knowing this about themselves.

S+R=O

Purpose:

To teach a formula that shows how students can change behaviors that have unhappy outcomes

Materials:

For each student:
- ☐ *S+R=O* (pages 104-105 or CD-Rom)
- ☐ Pen or pencil

ASCA Standards:

PERSONAL/SOCIAL DEVELOPMENT	
Standard B: Students will make decisions, set goals and take necessary action to achieve goals.	
PS:B1	Self-Knowledge Application
PS:B1.2	Understand consequences of decisions and choices

Directions:

S+R=O is a good formula to show students when discussing behavior.

    S (SITUATION)
+ R (REACTION OR RESPONSE TO THE SITUATION)
= O (OUTCOME)

Tell the students that if they don't like what is happening to them (outcome), they can change how they react (respond) to the situation to change the outcome.

Give the following examples:

Example #1:

Someone calls you a name (situation). You call him/her a name (react). You both get detentions or are sent to the office (outcome). Ask the students what they can do to get a better outcome. They may come up with things like *ignore the person,* or *tell an adult.* Ask what the outcome may be if they ignore the person or tell an adult. Point out that they wouldn't get detention or be sent to the office.

Example #2:

You have a lot of homework (situation). You don't do it (react). You get a failing grade. Ask what the students can do to get a better outcome. They have homework (situation). They complete it (react) and get a good grade (outcome).

Stress the need for students to be aware of how they react or respond to things. If they don't like what's happening to them, they can think of different ways to react or respond to get a better outcome.

The students practice this theory by writing an outcome for each *S+R=O* scenario.

☆ 103 ☆

S+R=O

Directions: Read each scenario and complete the outcomes for each reaction.

❶ **Situation:** Mary has basketball practice after school, but is tired and wants to go home.

React/Respond: Mary decides to skip practice and go home.

Outcome: _____

_____

React/Respond: Mary goes to practice even though she's tired.

Outcome: _____

_____

❷ **Situation:** Bill's mom has to work on Saturday. She asks Bill to clean the house. Bill starts to clean, but his friend stops over and asks him to go to the movies.

React/Respond: Bill goes to the movies without cleaning the house.

Outcome: _____

_____

React/Respond: Bill tells his friend he has to clean the house, and that maybe they can go to the movies the next day.

Outcome: _____

_____

❸ **Situation:** Sue didn't study for the test. She wants Nancy to let her copy from her. She vows the teacher won't catch them.

React/Respond: Nancy lets Sue copy.

Outcome: _____

_____

Ways To Amaze And Engage Middle School Students © 2009 Mar∗co Products, Inc. 1.800.448.2197

React/Respond: Nancy tells Sue she can't let her copy, but they can study together before the next test.

Outcome: _____

_____

❹ **Situation:** A teacher wrongly accuses Tim of talking while she was talking.

React/Respond: Tim yells, "I wasn't talking! You always blame me!

Outcome: _____

_____

React/Respond: Tim waits until after class and tells the teacher he knows she thinks he was talking, but he wasn't.

Outcome: _____

_____

❺ **Situation:** The grades on your report card are lower than you've ever received.

React/Respond: You hide it from your parents.

Outcome: _____

_____

React/Respond: You show your parents your report card, even though you know they'll be upset.

Outcome: _____

_____

Ways To Amaze And Engage Middle School Students © 2009 Mar∗co Products, Inc. 1.800.448.2197

Self-Esteem Wrinkle

Purpose:

To show students how negative remarks can affect themselves and others

Materials:

For each student:
☐ 4" x 6" piece of paper

ASCA Standards:

PERSONAL/SOCIAL DEVELOPMENT	
Standard A: Students will acquire the knowledge, attitudes and interpersonal skills to help them understand and respect self and others.	
PS:A1	Acquire Self-Knowledge
PS:A1.6	Distinguish between appropriate and inappropriate behavior

Directions:

Tell the students you're going to read a short story. Every time the students hear something negative in the story, they wrinkle part of their paper.

Read aloud:

One morning, Joe stayed in bed after his alarm went off. His mom yelled, "Something wrong with your hearing? Get up!" (wrinkle) Joe got up and went to eat breakfast. His little brother had eaten the rest of his favorite cereal. (wrinkle) Joe left to catch the bus, but ran back home to get his library book. His mom said, "Joe, you'd forget your head if it weren't attached." (wrinkle) On the bus, the boy in the next seat started to hit Joe's leg. (wrinkle) When Joe asked him to stop, the boy said, "What's wrong? Aren't you tough?" (wrinkle) At school, Joe couldn't open his locker. (wrinkle) He was late to homeroom. (wrinkle) His teacher gave him a tardy slip and told him a locker problem wasn't a good excuse for being late. (wrinkle) In math class, Joe discovered he'd done the wrong homework assignment. (wrinkle) At lunchtime, Joe's best friend decided to eat at another table. (wrinkle) During gym class, Joe was chosen last for the team. (wrinkle) At the end of the school day, some kids laughed at Joe's coat. (wrinkle) When he got home, his father and mother met him at the door. They said they'd received a letter from the principal, stating that Joe was chosen his school's *Student of the Month*. They told Joe they were proud of him.

Tell the students to try to smooth out the wrinkles. When it's obvious that they can't get all the wrinkles out of the paper, ask:

- What do the wrinkles signify?
- Even though positive things happen, why do wrinkles remain?
- What can you do to not put a wrinkle in someone's being?

Emphasize that negative comments are hurtful. With positive messages, the negatives may diminish, but they remain.

Ways To Amaze And Engage Middle School Students © 2009 Mar∗co Products, Inc. 1.800.448.2197

Simple Decision-Making Energizer

Purpose:

To promote a discussion on easy and more difficult decisions

Materials:

None required

ASCA Standards:

PERSONAL/SOCIAL DEVELOPMENT	
Standard B: Students will make decisions, set goals and take necessary action to achieve goals.	
PS:B1	Self-Knowledge Application
PS:B1.1	Use a decision-making and problem-solving model

Directions:

When beginning a decision-making lesson, have the students make simple decisions.

Ask:

Would you rather go to a fast-food restaurant that serves hamburgers (Point to the right side of the room.) *or pizza?* (Point to the left side.) *Tell the students to move to the side of their choice.*

Would you rather have a cell phone (Point to the right side.) *or an iPod®?* (Point to the left.) *The students move to the side of their choice.*

Continue, pointing to the side of the room to which the students should move.

- Which color do you like best—red or blue?
- Would you rather have an orange or an apple?
- Would you rather visit California or Florida?
- Would you rather go to the mountains or the ocean?
- Would you rather play/watch basketball or football?

- Which do you like better—snow or rain?
- Would you rather go skiing or surfing?
- Would you rather run or walk?
- Would you rather be with friends or family?
- Would you rather go on a roller coaster or a Ferris wheel?
- Would you rather go to an amusement park or a professional sports game?
- Would you rather travel by plane or car?
- Would you rather talk with someone or write to him/her?
- Which do you like better—social studies or science?

You may add to this list.

Discuss whether these decisions were easy or hard to make. For the most part, they're simple decisions that require little thought.

Discuss more difficult decisions and review the five steps in the decision-making process:

1. Clarify or define the decision.
2. Consider the choices.
3. Compare and weigh the options.
4. Choose the best option.
5. Carry out your plan.

Simple Story Energizer

Purpose:

To introduce motivating energizers for classroom use

Materials:

For the leader:
- ☐ *Energizer I* (pages 111-112 or CD-Rom) or *Energizer II* (pages 113-114 or CD-Rom)
- ☐ Prizes for winners

For each student:
- ☐ Paper
- ☐ Pencil

ASCA Standards:

PERSONAL/SOCIAL DEVELOPMENT	
Standard A: Students will acquire the knowledge, attitudes and interpersonal skills to help them understand and respect self and others.	
PS:A2	Acquire Interpersonal Skills
PS:A2.7	Know that communication involves speaking, listening and nonverbal behavior
Standard B: Students will make decisions, set goals and take necessary action to achieve goals.	
PS:B1	Self-Knowledge Application
PS:B1.7	Demonstrate a respect and appreciation for individual and cultural differences

Directions:

Tell the students you're going to read a poem that requires them to listen closely. Each student will add and subtract points when appropriate.

When you've finished reading the poem/energizer, the students total their scores. The student with the highest score wins a prize.

ENERGIZER I:

Get ready, class, to play a game
Where listening and math are one and the same.
You'll need paper and a pencil, too.
As we play this game, we'll focus on you.
You'll add up points and take away, too.
So listen carefully to what you must do.
The winner will walk away with a prize,
Get ready, get set, let me see your eyes.

If you ate breakfast this morning, give yourself two.
And if milk was a part, add one more for you.

If you're in the last desk at the end of the row,
You may add three as you watch your list grow.

If you did the homework that's due today,
Give yourself four and shout, "Hooray."

Take away three if you're wearing jeans.
But add two more if you're wearing green.

Take away one if your hair is blond.
But add two more if your hair is long.

Give one point for each button you have on you.
But take away one for each one that is blue.

If you have a zipper, you may add four.
If the zipper's on the side, you may add two more.

If you're wearing tennis shoes, add one to your sheet.
Take away two if sandals are on your feet.

If you have a sibling attending our school,
Give two points for each. Now isn't that cool?

If the sibling is male, though, take away one.
No offense boys. We're just having fun!

☆ **111** ☆

If you're wearing socks, give yourself three.
But take away two if they come to your knee.

Give one point for each textbook that's with you.
But if one is for science, take away two.

The letter A in your name, get two points for each one.
And add one more if you're having some fun!

If you're wearing a hoodie, add another four.
And if the hoodie is red, add two more.

Now is the time to total your score,
So add and subtract and we'll see who has more.

I hope you thought this game was just grand.
If you think you're the winner, would you please stand?

Ways To Amaze And Engage Middle School Students © 2009 Mar∗co Products, Inc. 1.800.448.2197

ENERGIZER II

It's time to play a game that is fun.
Where you add and subtract to see who has won.
If you listen carefully to what I will say,
One of you will leave with a grand prize today.
Have your paper and pencil ready to go.
Let us begin, now. On with the show!

Give yourself three points for being here today,
And add two more if your birthday's in May.

Take away one if your birthday's in December.
But add three if you were born in November!

What do you think? How's that for a start?
Now give yourself five if your hair has a part.

If you're wearing a belt, give yourself four.
If the belt is brown, you may add two more.

Take away two if your name starts with *D*.
If your name starts with *M*, you may add three.

If your very best friend is in here with you,
Lucky for you. You may add two.

If you sit in the last seat in the row,
Give yourself five and watch your list grow.

If you sit in the front seat, take away three.
And give yourself four if you need glasses to see.

Count up your buttons, give one point for each one.
Now this is my idea of fun!

If you're wearing socks, please add two.
But take away one if your socks are blue.

Let's take time now to tally our scores.
Once we do that, we'll continue with more.

Ways To Amaze And Engage Middle School Students © 2009 Mar∗co Products, Inc. 1.800.448.2197

Let's talk about interests, things that you like.
Add six if you rode to school on your bike.

Baseball, softball, soccer, and track,
Add one for each if that is your knack.

Football, basketball, and cross country, too,
Will earn you two each, IF the season is through.

If you're reading a book you particularly like,
Add five to your list to make your score spike.

But if it's fiction, take away four,
For more than 10 chapters, add three more.

If you're wearing a chain or necklace that shines,
Lucky for you. Give yourself nine!

If it's silver, take away two,
If it's gold, add one more for you.

Now let's take a good look at your shoes.
If they're red, give yourself two.

Take away three for shoes that you tie.
But if they have Velcro®, you may add five.

If your age is an even number of years,
Add four to your total and let out a cheer.

Take away five if your eyes are blue,
And add three if there's a dimple on you!

If you're writing your numbers with a pencil with lead,
You may add four to help you get ahead.

Add two more if your hair is black.
Subtract three if your shirt has words on the back.

Now I think we're just about done.
It's time to total your points and see who has won.
But wait … add five more if you think this was fun!

We are now finished. There isn't any more,
Would the student please stand who has the highest score?

Ways To Amaze And Engage Middle School Students © 2009 Mar∗co Products, Inc. 1.800.448.2197

Stick It To Me Name Game

Purpose:

To have students work together in a group and get to know each other

Materials:

For each student:
☐ Computer label

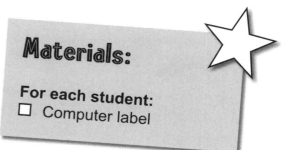

ASCA Standards:

PERSONAL/SOCIAL DEVELOPMENT	
Standard A: Students will acquire the knowledge, attitudes and interpersonal skills to help them understand and respect self and others.	
PS:A1	Acquire Self-Knowledge
PS:A1.9	Demonstrate cooperative behavior in groups

Directions:

Before presenting the activity, have everyone's name typed or written on individual self-adhesive labels. Computer labels work well.

The students stand in a circle.

Say that you're going to put another person's name on each student's back.

After each student has a label on his/her back, the students should find their name adhered to someone else's back. A student who finds his/her name should take it off that person's back, put it on his/her chest, and sit down.

The object of the game is for each student to find and remove his/her name while trying not to reveal the name on his/her own back. Students must keep moving and not stand with their back against the wall. The goal is to be one of the last students standing with a name on his/her back.

This is a good game to play when you first meet students, or students first meet each other.

Ways To Amaze And Engage Middle School Students © 2009 Mar✶co Products, Inc. 1.800.448.2197

Story A-Z

Purpose:

To have students work cooperatively

Materials:

None required

ASCA Standards:

PERSONAL/SOCIAL DEVELOPMENT	
Standard A: Students will acquire the knowledge, attitudes and interpersonal skills to help them understand and respect self and others.	
PS:A2	Acquire Interpersonal Skills
PS:A2.7	Know that communication involves speaking, listening and nonverbal behavior

Directions:

Assign each student a letter.

Tell the students they're going to work together and make up a story. The person with *A* will begin by using one word beginning with that letter. The student with *B* will go next. Each person must use only one word and the word must begin with the letter assigned to that student. The story must be constructed in alphabetical order.

For example:

Annie began climbing downward, eventually frantically going higher instead. Jumping keenly, landing more near open places. Quietly resting, sitting trustingly under vases without (e)xtra yellow zinnias.

Ways To Amaze Calendar

Purpose:

To help students develop a more positive attitude toward themselves

ASCA Standards:

PERSONAL/SOCIAL DEVELOPMENT	
Standard A: Students will acquire the knowledge, attitudes and interpersonal skills to help them understand and respect self and others.	
PS:A1	Acquire Self-Knowledge
PS:A1.1	Develop positive attitudes toward self as a unique and worthy person

Directions:

This activity is most successful when the classroom teacher is involved.

Give each student a copy of the *Ways To Amaze* Calendar at the beginning of the month.

Students fill in the dates above each task box. Once they complete the daily task, they cross out the box.

Give the classroom teacher a copy of the *Ways To Amaze* Calendar. Ask him/her to remind the students of each day's activity and, periodically, have the students describe their progress.

At the end of the month, students who have completed all activities in each box are entered in a prize drawing.

WAYS TO AMAZE CALENDAR

Say *hello* to someone you don't know.	Do something nice for someone.	Bring all your supplies to class.	Do something nice for a teacher.	Help out at home.	Wear a favorite piece of clothing.	Give yourself three positive messages.

Get to know someone new.	Eat lunch with someone you don't know well.	Eat something healthy.	Write to or talk with an old friend.	Smile at everyone you see.	Offer to help someone.	Try something new or that challenges you.

Send someone a card.	Let someone cut in front of you in the lunch line.	Tell someone something you're proud of.	Give someone a hug.	Tell your parents something you like about them.	Tell a friend something you like about him/her.	Take a walk or ride a bike.

Do something nice for yourself.	Clean out your locker.	Write down a goal for this school year.	Write a *thank-you* note to someone.	Listen to your favorite song.	Start reading a new book.	Clean your room.

☆ 118 ☆

CLASSROOM GAMES

Pair, Share, And Care Card Game

Purpose:

To encourage students to recognize and discuss their feelings, practice good listening skills, and show empathy

Materials:

For the leader:
- ☐ *Feeling-Word Cards* (pages 122-125 or CD-Rom)
- ☐ Scissors

ASCA Standards:

PERSONAL/SOCIAL DEVELOPMENT	
Standard A: Students will acquire the knowledge, attitudes and interpersonal skills to help them understand and respect self and others.	
PS:A1	Acquire Self-Knowledge
PS:A1.5	Identify and express feelings

Number of Players:

Four or more. Two players if some of the pairs are removed from the deck of cards

Directions:

Reproduce the cards. Cut them apart. Shuffle and deal the cards until there are no cards left.

Players may look at their cards, but may not show them to other players.

Players begin by laying down any pair of *Feeling-Word Cards* they have.

A player who lays down a pair must describe a time he/she felt the emotion stated on those cards.

When all pairs have been laid down, the first player fans out his/her remaining cards, face-down. The person on the left draws one of them. The first player picks up his/her cards.

A player who draws a card that makes a pair lays the pair down and describes a time he/she felt that way. If the card drawn does not make a pair, the card is kept in the player's hand. That player fans his/her cards to the player on his/her left and the game continues.

The group plays until one person is left with the *CARE* card. That person wins the game.

Ways To Amaze And Engage Middle School Students © 2009 Mar*co Products, Inc. 1.800.448.2197

Happy	Happy
Angry	Angry
Proud	Proud
Discouraged	Discouraged
Hopeful	Hopeful
Content	Content
Ecstatic	Ecstatic

Hurt	Hurt
Excited	Excited
Surprised	Surprised
Anxious	Anxious
Worried	Worried
Confident	Confident
Confused	Confused

Frustrated	Frustrated
Lonely	Lonely
Overwhelmed	Overwhelmed
Miserable	Miserable
Annoyed	Annoyed
Envious	Envious
Scared	Scared

Irritated	Irritated
Appreciated	Appreciated
Distraught	Distraught
Silly	Silly
CARE	

Ways To Amaze And Engage Middle School Students © 2009 Mar⋆co Products, Inc. 1.800.448.2197

Fishing For Feelings Card Game

Purpose:

To help students identify and express feelings

ASCA Standards:

PERSONAL/SOCIAL DEVELOPMENT	
Standard A: Students will acquire the knowledge, attitudes and interpersonal skills to help them understand and respect self and others.	
PS:A1	Acquire Self-Knowledge
PS:A1.5	Identify and express feelings

Number of Players:

2–5

Directions:

Reproduce four sets of *Fishing For Feelings* cards. Cut them apart. This game is played like the card game *Go Fish*.

Deal each player five cards.

The rest of the cards are turned face-down or spread out face-down in the center of the table.

The first player asks another player for a certain *Fishing For Feelings Card*. If the player who was asked has that card, he/she must give it to the person who requested it. The first player continues and asks a different player for a specific *Fishing For Feelings Card*. Play continues until the asked player does not have the requested card and says "Fish For Feelings." The player then picks a card from the extra cards on the table. The next player takes his/her turn.

A player who collects four of one *Fishing For Feelings* Cards lays those cards down (when it is his/her turn) and describes a time he/she felt the emotion on the card.

The winner is the first person who has no cards left.

Other players may then share their hands and describe times they felt the emotions stated on their cards.

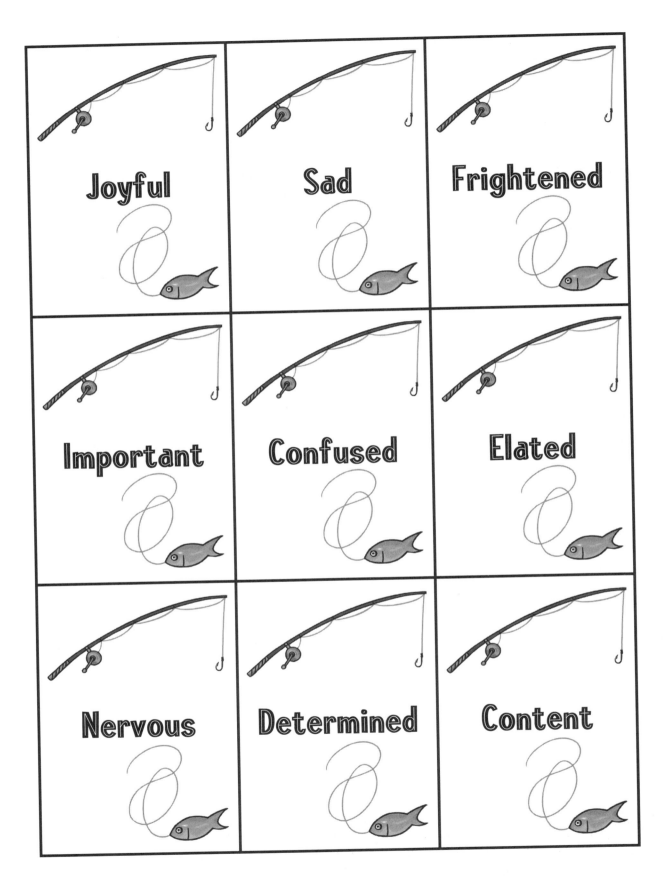

Joyful

Sad

Frightened

Important

Confused

Elated

Nervous

Determined

Content

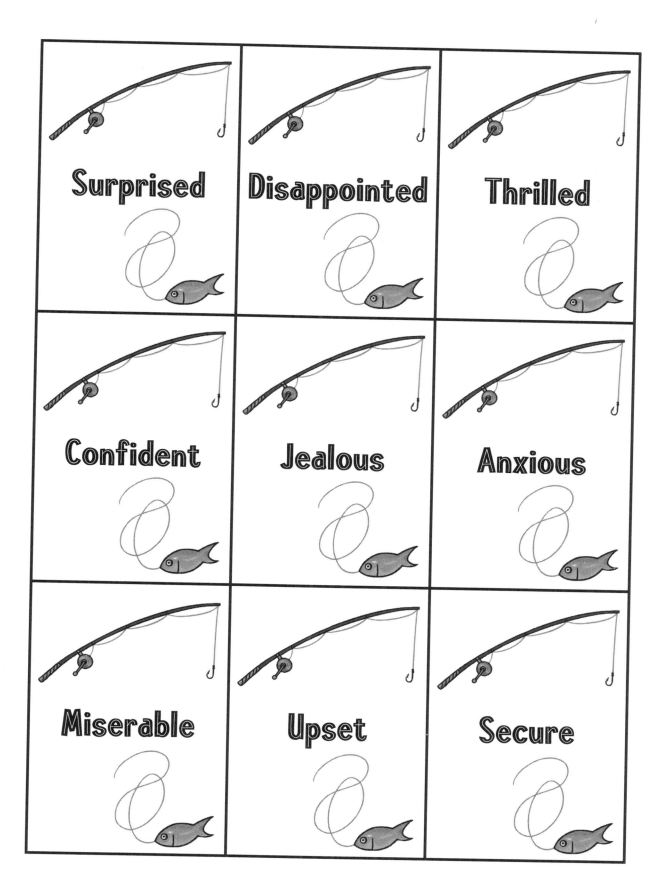

Surprised

Disappointed

Thrilled

Confident

Jealous

Anxious

Miserable

Upset

Secure

Fly Swatter I

Purpose:

To review listening skills and bullying and decision-making roles

ASCA Standards:

PERSONAL/SOCIAL DEVELOPMENT	
Standard A: Students will acquire the knowledge, attitudes and interpersonal skills to help them understand and respect self and others.	
PS:A2	Acquire Interpersonal Skills
PS:A2.6	Use effective communications skills
Standard B: Students will make decisions, set goals and take necessary action to achieve goals.	
PS:B1	Self-Knowledge Application
PS:B1.2	Understand consequences of decisions and choices
Standard C: Students will understand safety and survival skills.	
PS:C1	Acquire Personal Safety Skills
PS:C1.2	Learn about the relationship between rules, laws, safety and the protection of rights of the individual

Number of Players:

Classroom

Directions:

(*Note*: This is a good game to use when reviewing terms and definitions.)

On the board, draw circles for each term the students are to review. Write each term in a separate circle.

Ways To Amaze And Engage Middle School Students © 2009 Mar✶co Products, Inc. 1.800.448.2197

An example from a small-group counseling or classroom program on bullying could be:

Focus, Accept, Give Feedback, Aggressive, Passive, Assertive, Ringleader Bully, Victim, Assistant Bullies, Reinforcers, Bystanders, Defender, Automatic Decision, Daily Decision, Major Decision

Divide the students into two teams. A student from each team comes to the board. The first student to cover with a fly swatter the circle containing the correct answer earns a point. The students sit down and the next two students come to the board. Repeat this procedure until everyone has had a turn. The team with the most points wins.

Examples of questions using the words from the sample above:

- Target of the bully (victim)
- Brushing your teeth every morning (daily decision)
- Respectfully let others know what you want or need (assertive)
- Nod or smile when someone is talking (accept)
- People who laugh when they see someone bullying (reinforcers)
- Make eye contact, leaning toward the speaker (focus)
- Where to go to college (major decision)
- Do and say nothing, even though you don't like what's happening (passive)
- Main bully (ringleader bully)
- Ask a question or comment about what someone said (give feedback)
- Do nothing when witnessing bullying (bystanders)
- Yell, scream, and/or make fists about what you don't like (aggressive)
- Help a bully make fun of a victim (assistant bullies)
- Helps the victim or reports bullying to an adult (defender)
- Getting up in the morning (automatic decision)

Fly Swatter II

Purpose:

To identify feeling words from their meanings

Materials:

For the leader:
- ☐ 2 fly swatters
- ☐ Board and marker

ASCA Standards:

PERSONAL/SOCIAL DEVELOPMENT	
Standard A: Students will acquire the knowledge, attitudes and interpersonal skills to help them understand and respect self and others.	
PS:A1	Acquire Self-Knowledge
PS:A1.5	Identify and express feelings

Number of Players:

Classroom

Directions:

Write each of the following *feeling words* in a separate circle.

> Miserable, Confused, Disappointed, Blissful, Frustrated, Hurt, Envious, Proud, Content, Furious, Exhausted, Eager, Lonely, Supported

Divide the students into two teams. Have one student from each team come to the board. Give each student a fly swatter. The first student to cover the circle with a fly swatter, that has the correct answer, gets a point. They sit down and the next two students come up. Repeat this procedure this until everyone has a turn. The team with the most points wins.

Questions using the feeling words:

- Drained, very tired (exhausted)
- Very mad (furious)

- Extremely sad (miserable)
- Ecstatic (blissful)
- Jealous (envious)
- By yourself, left out (lonely)
- Trying without success to do something (frustrated)
- Excited (eager)
- Helping someone or being helped (supported)
- When something anticipated doesn't happen (disappointed)
- Valuing self and/or accomplishments (proud)
- Calm (content)
- Perplexed, mixed up (confused)
- Physical or mental suffering (hurt)

Drug and Alcohol Information Jeopardy

Purpose:

To present and review facts about drugs and alcohol

Materials:

For the leader:
- ☐ 8½" X 11" sheets of red, green, pink, yellow, and blue paper for writing or printing the question cards (included on CD-Rom)

ASCA Standards:

PERSONAL/SOCIAL DEVELOPMENT	
Standard C: Students will understand safety and survival skills.	
PS:C1	Acquire Personal Safety Skills
PS:C1.8	Learn about the emotional and physical dangers of substance use and abuse

Number of Players:

Classroom

Directions:

This game has five categories. Each column includes the section title, plus point amounts in this order—100, 200, 300, 400, 500. Use a separate color for each category. The sheets may be taped on the board. It should look like this:

RED PAPER	GREEN PAPER	PINK PAPER	YELLOW PAPER	BLUE PAPER
GIVE THE NUMBER	NAME THE DRUG	EFFECTS	GIVE THE PERCENTAGE	MISC. FACTS
100	100	100	100	100
200	200	200	200	200
300	300	300	300	300
400	400	400	400	400
500	500	500	500	500

Below is a sample of what can be written on the back of each paper in each category. These questions have also been provided on the CD to print on colored paper. Remove a selected category from the board, turn the paper over, and ask the question on the back.

	RED PAPER	GREEN PAPER	PINK PAPER	YELLOW PAPER	BLUE PAPER
100 →	How many people who try to quit smoking actually succeed? (1 in 10)	This drug causes liver damage, hypertension, anemia, and contributes to half of all motor vehicle accidents. (alcohol)	Lung cancer and emphysema are effects of what drug? (nicotine)	The percentage of smokers who start smoking in their teens. (30%)	Young smokers are how much more likely than young non-smokers to smoke pot and become addicted to drugs? (100 times)
200 →	It's hardest to quit smoking for someone who starts smoking before this age. (21)	These extremely dangerous drugs include hair spray and gasoline. (inhalants)	This drug is the leading cause of death for teens in auto accidents. (alcohol)	The percentage of smokers who started smoking before the age of 17 and say they regret smoking. (80–90%)	These stop bone growth in teenagers. (steroids)
300 →	Using inhalants has been associated with irreversible brain damage. Using inhalants even ___ time(s) can kill. (one)	This powerful drug is absorbed through the lungs and into the bloodstream. (nicotine)	This drug damages memory, problem-solving, and learning ability. (marijuana)	The percentage of high school students who have tried alcohol. (75%)	*DAILY DOUBLE* Name three drug-withdrawal symptoms. (aching, sweating, fever, shaking, chills)
400 →	Nicotine reaches the brain in how many seconds? (8)	An artificial version of a hormone (steroid)	People use these to build muscles. But they can cause cancer, heart attacks, strokes, balding. (steroids)	The percentage of Americans who don't drink. (33%)	This causes cancer of the mouth, pharynx, larynx, and esophagus. (chewing tobacco)

☆ 135 ☆

500 →	How many chemicals in marijuana affect the brain? (more than 400)	This is the most commonly used hallucinogen. (marijuana)	DAILY DOUBLE Name a drug that causes serious, lasting psychiatric problems. (LSD)	The percentage of youth who will continue to smoke and die early due to a smoking-related disease. (70%)	Name three ingredients in cigarettes. (nicotine, cyanide, carbon monoxide, formaldehyde, methanol, acetone, tar)

Divide the students into two teams. Team A has one person choose a category and answer the question. If he/she answers correctly the point value is added to the team's score. Then it's Team B's turn. If the student on team A misses the question, team B has an opportunity to answer and earn the points. After team B answers correctly, the next person on Team A selects a category and answers. When the board is cleared, the team with the most points wins.

The Strongest Link

Purpose:

To review life skills

ASCA Standards:

Materials:

For the leader:
- ☐ Board and marker
- ☐ 6 notebooks
- ☐ 6 pencils

PERSONAL/SOCIAL DEVELOPMENT	
Standard A: Students will acquire the knowledge, attitudes and interpersonal skills to help them understand and respect self and others.	
PS:A1	Acquire Self-Knowledge
PS:A1.2	Identify values, attitudes and beliefs
PS:A1.5	Identify and express feelings
PS:A1.12	Identify and recognize changing family roles
PS:A2	Acquire Interpersonal Skills
PS:A2.2	Respect alternative points of view
Standard B: Students will make decisions, set goals and take necessary action to achieve goals.	
PS:B1	Self-Knowledge Application
PS:B1.4	Develop effective coping skills for dealing with problems
PS:B1.11	Use persistence and perseverance in acquiring knowledge and skills
Standard C: Students will understand safety and survival skills.	
PS:C1	Acquire Personal Safety Skills
PS:C1.10	Learn techniques for managing stress and conflict
PS:C1.11	Learn coping skills for managing life events

Number of Players:

Classroom

Directions:

Divide the students into Team A and Team B. Choose three students from each side to come to the front of the room to answer questions.

Give each student a notebook and a pencil in which to record his/her answers.

The leader asks a question (see sample questions below), and each student records his/her answer in his/her notebook.

Ask the first person on Team A to show the answer he/she recorded. If the answer is correct, Team A gets two points. Record the points on the board.

If the answer is incorrect, the first person on Team B may answer the question. If he/she answers correctly, Team B earns one point. It's recorded on the board.

If the question is missed, it goes to the second person on Team A. Once the question is answered correctly, each person who had the correct answer written down gets one point.

Follow this alternating procedure and record the points on the board until someone answers correctly. If none of the six contestants answers correctly, ask the audience. Begin with the team that first answered the question.

The team of the audience member who answers correctly gets one point.

Begin the next question with Team B.

After all six students have had a turn to answer first, have the contestants write down the name of someone whom they want to sit down. The person with the most votes must go back to his/her seat.

The notebook is given to the team member chosen to replace the person who sat down.

This is a good game for review.

Sample decision-making questions:

- Name two things that influence decisions (personal opinion, friend's opinion, parent's opinion, TV, magazines, costs, etc.)
- What word describes when a person says or does something he/she doesn't believe in? (hypocrisy)
- Name five C's in decision making (clarify, consider, compare, choose, carry out)

Questions for coping with anxiety:

- What is *anxiety?* (nervous, uptight feeling)
- What can you do when you feel anxious? (breathe deeply, visualize, think positively, relax muscles)
- What can you tell yourself if you're thinking negative thoughts? (cancel, cancel; I can do it; I will do it)

Ways To Amaze And Engage Middle School Students © 2009 Mar*co Products, Inc. 1.800.448.2197

Questions for coping with anger:

- Anger is one letter away from what word? (danger)
- Give the three rules for handling anger. (can't hurt yourself, can't hurt others, can't destroy property)
- Give three healthy ways to handle anger (self-talk, talk with someone, play, sports, write, music, etc.)

Questions for communication skills:

- What are the two types of communication? (verbal and non-verbal)
- Non-verbal communication refers to _____. (body language, expressions, gestures)
- Name two forms of verbal communication (talking, writing, music)
- What are two components of effective listening? (sending and receiving)
- What is one thing an active listener will do? (focus, accept, give feedback)
- What is one thing that shows a person is not listening? (no eye contact, turn away from speaker, interrupt, laugh at the wrong time)
- What is one specific thing a person can do to avoid misunderstandings? (ask questions, paraphrase, be specific, make sure verbal and non-verbal messages are consistent)

Questions for social skills:

- Give an example of an open-ended question. (tell me about, what do you think about, how do you feel about)
- Give an example of a closed-ended question. (do you like, did you go)
- What is one way to start a conversation with someone you don't know? (smile and say, "Hi"; ask a question; give a compliment; request or offer help; talk about the weather)
- How can you end a conversation? (find a natural place to stop, break eye contact, move toward the door, shake hands)

Questions for assertiveness:

- This means calmly standing up for yourself or expressing your thoughts/feelings without hurting others. (being assertive)
- This means accepting things without objecting or resisting, even though you strongly disagree. (being passive)
- This means acting in a way that violates other people's rights. You might overreact, get in someone's face, be forceful and loud. (being aggressive)
- Give an example of a time you would be assertive. (returning defective merchandise; getting short-changed; someone cuts in front of you in the lunch line)
- Name two ways to be assertive. (eye contact, facial expression, body matches what you're saying, maintain the right distance, fluent speech)

☆ **139** ☆

COUNSELOR/ TEACHER IDEAS

Bingo Boards

Purpose:

Concept review

ASCA Standards:

These will depend on lesson that will be taught.

Materials:

For the leader:
- ☐ *Bingo Board* (page 143 or CD-Rom)
- ☐ *Bingo Numbers* (page 144 or CD-Rom)
- ☐ Scissors
- ☐ Container
- ☐ Pen

For each student:
- ☐ *Bingo Board* (page 143 or CD-Rom)
- ☐ Pen or marker

Directions:

When reviewing or reinforcing a lesson or concept, Bingo is fun to play.

Customize the Bingo game to fit your lesson. Open-ended questions, definitions, and vocabulary words are a few ways to use this activity. Reproduce the *Bingo Board* and fill in the boxes on one board. Reproduce this sample board for each student.

Cut apart the *Bingo Numbers* and place them in a container.

Give each student a completed *Bingo Board*.

Students create their own board by randomly filling in numbers in the upper right corner of each square. Make sure they make the columns 1–15, 16–30, 31–45, 46–60, and 61–75.

When a number is called, a student who has that number answers what is in the box and crosses out the square. Five in a row, or any combination you choose, is Bingo!

Ways To Amaze And Engage Middle School Students © 2009 Mar⋆co Products, Inc. 1.800.448.2197

BINGO BOARD

B 1–15	I 16–30	N 31–45	G 46–60	O 61–75

BINGO NUMBERS

B-1	I-16	N-31	G-46	O-61
B-2	I-17	N-32	G-47	O-62
B-3	I-18	N-33	G-48	O-63
B-4	I-19	N-34	G-49	O-64
B-5	I-20	N-35	G-50	O-65
B-6	I-21	N-36	G-51	O-66
B-7	I-22	N-37	G-52	O-67
B-8	I-23	N-38	G-53	O-68
B-9	I-24	N-39	G-54	O-69
B-10	I-25	N-40	G-55	O-70
B-11	I-26	N-41	G-56	O-71
B-12	I-27	N-42	G-57	O-72
B-13	I-28	N-43	G-58	O-73
B-14	I-29	N-44	G-59	O-74
B-15	I-30	N-45	G-60	O-75

Conflict-Resolution Plan

Purpose:

To develop a conflict-resolution plan using the letters in the school mascot's name

Materials:

For the leader:
☐ Tagboard or colored paper

ASCA Standards:

PERSONAL/SOCIAL DEVELOPMENT	
Standard B: Students will make decisions, set goals and take necessary action to achieve goals.	
PS:B1	Self-Knowledge Application
PS:B1.1	Use a decision-making and problem-solving model
PS:B1.4	Develop effective coping skills for dealing with problems

Directions:

Using each letter in your school mascot's name, write a statement that deals with solving conflicts peacefully. Reproduce the plan on tagboard or colored paper and post it throughout the school.

An example for a school whose mascot is Ravens:

R esolution is our goal in dealing with conflict.

A lways use "I" statements when mediating conflicts.

V oice your point of view.

E valuate alternatives for resolving the conflict.

N ever ignore one side of the story.

S hare how you feel.

Ways To Amaze And Engage Middle School Students © 2009 Mar∗co Products, Inc. 1.800.448.2197

100 Grand Payday

Purpose:

To recognize students who do well

Materials:

For the leader:
- ☐ Note paper
- ☐ Ribbon
- ☐ Pen

For each student:
- ☐ 100 Grand® candy bar or Payday® candy bar

ASCA Standards:

PERSONAL/SOCIAL DEVELOPMENT	
Standard A: Students will acquire the knowledge, attitudes and interpersonal skills to help them understand and respect self and others.	
PS:A1	Acquire Self-Knowledge
PS:A1.1	Develop positive attitudes toward self as a unique and worthy person

Directions:

To recognize an accomplishment, give the student a *100 Grand* or *Payday* candy bar wrapped in a congratulatory note. The note may look something like this:

Congratulations on your 100 Grand Payday! You earned this award because of all the hard work you've done this nine weeks.

Alternative:

Give the candy bars to recognize *Students Of The Month* or students who do more than expected. It's a fun way to reward students.

Ways To Amaze And Engage Middle School Students © 2009 Mar✶co Products, Inc. 1.800.448.2197

Positive Attitude Week

Purpose:

To encourage students to be more positive with others and with themselves

Materials:

For the students:
- ☐ Rewards
- ☐ Treats

ASCA Standards:

PERSONAL/SOCIAL DEVELOPMENT	
Standard A: Students will acquire the knowledge, attitudes and interpersonal skills to help them understand and respect self and others.	
PS:A2	Acquire Interpersonal Skills
PS:A2.3	Recognize, accept, respect and appreciate individual differences

Directions:

Designate *Positive Attitude Week* to encourage students to be more positive with others and with themselves.

Each day's theme encourages students to be positive.

Monday *Catch Someone Being Positive Day*. Teachers hand out rewards to students they catch being positive.

Tuesday *Say Something Nice to Others Day*. There will be no put-downs.

Wednesday *Student Appreciation Day*. Give treats or gifts to show students they're appreciated. Pencils or pins with the school name are nice.

Thursday *Staff Appreciation Day*. Staff members get gifts from the administration to let them know they're appreciated. Students write notes to tell favorite staff members why they're appreciated.

Friday *Help Someone Out Day*. Students assist someone in some way.

Daily announcements talk about the day's theme and include a quote like:

- "One of the greatest gifts is the ability to give." ~Unknown
- "That best portion of a good man's life, His little, nameless, unremembered acts of kindness and of love." ~William Wordsworth
- "The welfare of each is bound up in the welfare of all." ~Helen Keller:
- "It's nice to be important, but it is more important to be nice." ~John M. Templeton
- "You don't have to blow out another person's candle to make yours glow brighter." ~Unknown
- "There is no time limit on kindness." ~Donna B. Forrest
- "If you want to lift yourself up, lift up someone else." ~Booker T. Washington
- "People who matter are well aware that everyone else does, too." ~Malcolm S. Forbes
- "No one can make you feel inferior without your consent." ~Eleanor Roosevelt
- "Nothing improves my hearing better than praise." ~Unknown
- "Some people look at a glass and say that it is half-empty. Others look at the same glass and say that it is half-full." ~Unknown
- "People are lonely because they build walls instead of bridges." ~Joseph Fort Newton
- "Tact is rubbing out another's mistakes, instead of rubbing them in." ~Marvin J. Ashton
- "If we must disagree, let's disagree without being disagreeable." ~Lyndon Johnson

The quotes may also be used in class. Have the students write about what they think the quote means, then share their thoughts. The students can make signs with these quotes and distribute them around the school.

Ways To Amaze And Engage Middle School Students © 2009 Mar∗co Products, Inc. 1.800.448.2197

Sticky Notes

Purpose:

To suggest a creative way for students to ask and answer questions

ASCA Standards:

These will depend on lesson that will be taught

Directions:

One good way to brainstorm or ask or answer questions without singling students out is to use sticky notes.

Ask a specific question. Have the students write one answer on each sticky note and put the notes on the designated board or chart.

For example:

Divide the class into thirds. Have one-third of the students write suggestions/ideas about "Things We Like About School" on their notes and put them on the board under that title.

Have the second group of the students write suggestions/ideas about "Things We Don't Like About School" and put their notes under that title.

The last group will write suggestions/ideas about "Suggestions On How To Make Our School Better" and put their ideas under that title.

Read the students' responses.

Have the students discuss what was written and add anything they feel is missing.

Materials:

For the leader:
☐ Sticky notes or Post-It® notes
☐ Board

Ways To Amaze And Engage Middle School Students © 2009 Mar*co Products, Inc. 1.800.448.2197

Suggested topics:

- Things Bullies Do/Where Bullying Happens/Why Bullies Bully
- At the beginning of the school year: Things I Hope To Learn This Year/Things I Hope Won't Happen This Year/Things I Want To Accomplish This Year
- At the end of the school year: What I Liked Best About This Year/Things I Didn't Like About This Year/Changes That Happened This Year
- Evaluate lessons by having the students write: What They Liked Best About The Lesson, What They Liked Least About The Lesson/How The Lesson Can Be Improved

Quiet Class

Purpose:

To introduce class-quieting techniques

Materials:

None required

ASCA Standards:

PERSONAL/SOCIAL DEVELOPMENT	
Standard A: Students will acquire the knowledge, attitudes and interpersonal skills to help them understand and respect self and others.	
PS:A2	Acquire Interpersonal Skills
PS:A2.7	Know that communication involves speaking, listening and nonverbal behavior

Directions:

When trying to quiet the class, say quietly:

- If you can hear me, clap twice.
- If you can hear me, clap three times.
- If you can hear me, clap four times.
- If you can hear me, clap five times.

As the students hear what the teacher/counselor is saying, they start to clap.

Stop speaking once everyone is clapping and the class is quiet. Begin your lesson.

Ways To Amaze And Engage Middle School Students © 2009 Mar★co Products, Inc. 1.800.448.2197

Staff Member Brag Bag

Purpose:

To have students write positive messages to staff members

Materials:

For the leader:
☐ Large bag
☐ Optional: *Brag Bag Form* (page 153 or CD-Rom)

ASCA Standards:

PERSONAL/SOCIAL DEVELOPMENT	
Standard A: Students will acquire the knowledge, attitudes and interpersonal skills to help them understand and respect self and others.	
PS:A2	Acquire Interpersonal Skills
PS:A2.3	Recognize, accept, respect and appreciate individual differences

Directions:

Tell the students there will be Brag Bag for staff members in the guidance office. Obtain a large bag and label it Brag Bag.

Students may write a positive comment to let any staff member know how much he/she is appreciated or to thank a staff member for something. They must sign what they write before putting it in the *Brag Bag*. The counselor will make sure staff members receive positive comments that are in the bag for them.

(*Note*: You may reproduce the *Brag Bag Form* and have students use it to compliment a staff member.)

Ways To Amaze And Engage Middle School Students © 2009 Mar✶co Products, Inc. 1.800.448.2197

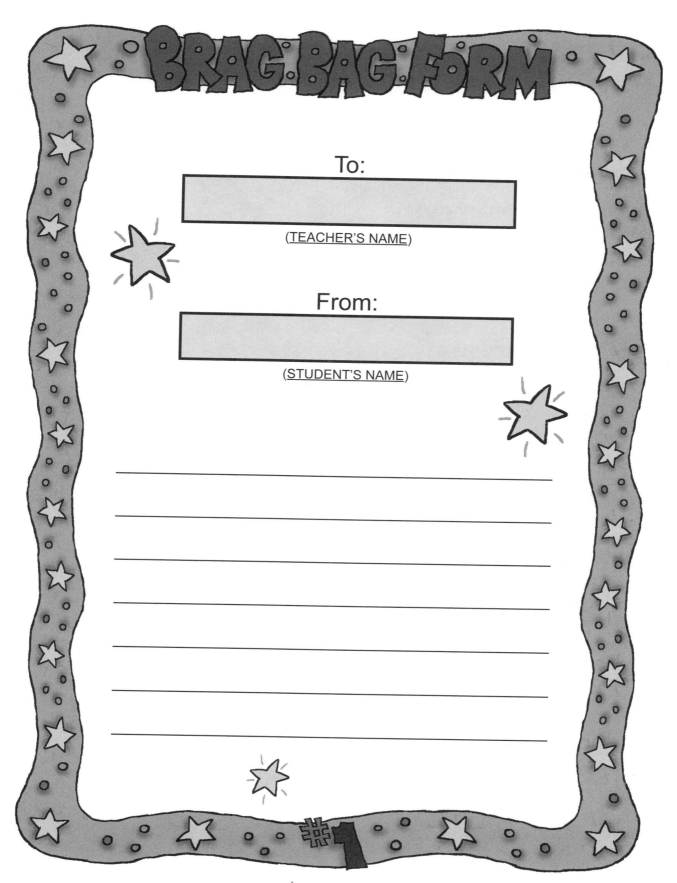

BRAG BAG FORM

To:

(TEACHER'S NAME)

From:

(STUDENT'S NAME)

Ways To Amaze And Engage Middle School Students © 2009 Mar★co Products, Inc. 1.800.448.2197

Test-Survival Kit

Purpose:

To introduce test-taking strategies

Materials:

For each student:
- ☐ Pencil
- ☐ Penny
- ☐ Star sticker
- ☐ Mini pretzels
- ☐ Small box of raisins
- ☐ Confetti
- ☐ *Test-Survival Tools* (page 155 or CD-Rom)
- ☐ Plastic bag

ASCA Standards:

ACADEMIC IMPROVEMENT	
Standard B: Students will complete school with the academic preparation essential to choose from a wide range of substantial post- secondary options, including college.	
A:B1	Improve Learning
A:B1.3	Apply the study skills necessary for academic success at each level

Directions:

Before testing, give each student a Test-Survival Kit consisting of a copy of *Test-Survival Tools*, a pencil, penny, mini pretzels, star sticker, small box of raisins, and confetti in a plastic bag.

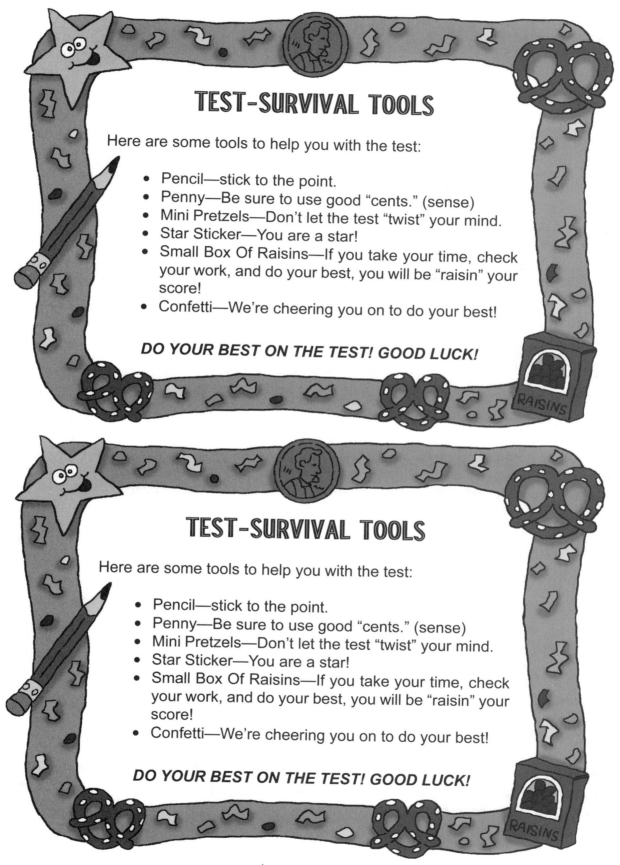

TEST-SURVIVAL TOOLS

Here are some tools to help you with the test:

- Pencil—stick to the point.
- Penny—Be sure to use good "cents." (sense)
- Mini Pretzels—Don't let the test "twist" your mind.
- Star Sticker—You are a star!
- Small Box Of Raisins—If you take your time, check your work, and do your best, you will be "raisin" your score!
- Confetti—We're cheering you on to do your best!

DO YOUR BEST ON THE TEST! GOOD LUCK!

TEST-SURVIVAL TOOLS

Here are some tools to help you with the test:

- Pencil—stick to the point.
- Penny—Be sure to use good "cents." (sense)
- Mini Pretzels—Don't let the test "twist" your mind.
- Star Sticker—You are a star!
- Small Box Of Raisins—If you take your time, check your work, and do your best, you will be "raisin" your score!
- Confetti—We're cheering you on to do your best!

DO YOUR BEST ON THE TEST! GOOD LUCK!

Ways To Amaze And Engage Middle School Students © 2009 Mar*co Products, Inc. 1.800.448.2197

Ways To Put Students Into Groups

Purpose:

To let students experience working with other students in group activities

ASCA Standards:

PERSONAL/SOCIAL DEVELOPMENT	
Standard A: Students will acquire the knowledge, attitudes and interpersonal skills to help them understand and respect self and others	
PS:A1	Acquire Self-Knowledge
PS:A1.9	Demonstrate cooperative behavior in groups

Count Off

The most common way to put students into groups is to have the students count off, beginning with *1* and ending with the number equal to the number of groups you want to have. For example, count from 1 to 4 for four groups. When everyone in the classroom has counted, put the 1s in a group, the 2s in a group, etc.

Hum A Song

Have each student draw a slip of paper listing a familiar song and start humming the song. When they find other students humming the same song, they join together.

Continue until everyone has found the students humming his/her song.

When preparing this activity, make four or five slips of paper listing the same song. Do this for as many groups as you want to have.

Craft Sticks

Have as many craft sticks in a can as you have students. Color the ends of each craft stick. Each student picks a stick without seeing the color. Group the students according to the color of the stick they chose.

Ways To Amaze And Engage Middle School Students © 2009 Mar✶co Products, Inc. 1.800.448.2197

Animal Sounds

On each slip of paper, write the name of an animal. Make four or five slips of paper for the same animal, depending on how large you want your groups to be. Students walk around the room, making the sound made by the animal listed on their paper. When they find other students making that same sound, they join together and form a group.

Gem Stones

Fill a box with packing peanuts. Add colored gemstones from a craft store. Have enough of each color to form as many groups as you need. For example, if you want five in a group, put in five clear stones, five pink, five blue, five green, and five red. Have each student reach into the box, without looking, and find a "jewel." Once everyone has a stone, have the students form groups according to the color of their gemstones.

Miniature Candy Bar

Put miniature candy bars in a box full of packing peanuts. Have enough of each kind of candy bar for as many groups as you plan to have. Students reach into the box without looking and take a candy bar. When everyone has a candy bar, the students form groups according to the kind of candy they took from the box.

Ways To Amaze And Engage Middle School Students © 2009 Mar✳co Products, Inc. 1.800.448.2197

FORMS

Classroom-Guidance Evaluation

Purpose:

To have students evaluate a classroom-guidance presentation

Materials:

For each student:
- ☐ *Classroom-Guidance Evaluation* (page 161 or CD-Rom)
- ☐ Pencil

ASCA Standards:

PERSONAL/SOCIAL DEVELOPMENT	
Standard A: Students will acquire the knowledge, attitudes and interpersonal skills to help them understand and respect self and others	
PS:A1	Acquire Self-Knowledge
PS:A1.2	Identify values, attitudes and beliefs

Directions:

Review the directions for the *Classroom Guidance Evaluation*. Collect and tabulate the completed forms.

CLASSROOM-GUIDANCE EVALUATION

Directions: On a scale of 1–5, with 1 being *low*, 3 *average*, and 5 *high*, evaluate our classroom lessons. Circle a number to evaluate each statement.

I liked the activities.

1........2........3........4........5
LOW — AVERAGE — HIGH

I learned something new.

1........2........3........4........5
LOW — AVERAGE — HIGH

The class worked together.

1........2........3........4........5
LOW — AVERAGE — HIGH

Behavior of class

1........2........3........4........5
LOW — AVERAGE — HIGH

Knowledge of facilitator

1........2........3........4........5
LOW — AVERAGE — HIGH

Group cooperation

1........2........3........4........5
LOW — AVERAGE — HIGH

Made learning fun

1........2........3........4........5
LOW — AVERAGE — HIGH

COMMENTS:

_____

_____

_____

_____

_____

_____

Ways To Amaze And Engage Middle School Students © 2009 Mar∗co Products, Inc. 1.800.448.2197

Documentation

Purpose:

To provide an accurate and easy-to-use method for recording student information

Materials:

For the leader:
☐ *Documentation Forms* (pages 163-164 or CD-Rom)

Directions:

Print or reproduce a *Documentation Form*. Keep these cards in a file folder.

There are two types of forms included:

1. The front of one type has a dated calendar on which you may check a specified problem under P (personal), A (academic), C (career), or S (social). Additional comments/notes may be written on the back of the form.

2. The front of the other type of card has a dated calendar on which you may check a specified problem as P (personal) or G (general). Additional comments/notes may be written on the back of the form.

Name: _____ Grade: _____
                                                    Date: _____

Mark with "P" for *Personal*, "A" for *Academic*, "C" for *Career*, "S" for *Social*

AUG	SEPT	OCT	NOV	DEC	JAN	FEB	MAR	APR	MAY	JUNE	JULY
1	1	1	1	1	1	1	1	1	1	1	1
2	2	2	2	2	2	2	2	2	2	2	2
3	3	3	3	3	3	3	3	3	3	3	3
4	4	4	4	4	4	4	4	4	4	4	4
5	5	5	5	5	5	5	5	5	5	5	5
6	6	6	6	6	6	6	6	6	6	6	6
7	7	7	7	7	7	7	7	7	7	7	7
8	8	8	8	8	8	8	8	8	8	8	8
9	9	9	9	9	9	9	9	9	9	9	9
10	10	10	10	10	10	10	10	10	10	10	10
11	11	11	11	11	11	11	11	11	11	11	11
12	12	12	12	12	12	12	12	12	12	12	12
13	13	13	13	13	13	13	13	13	13	13	13
14	14	14	14	14	14	14	14	14	14	14	14
15	15	15	15	15	15	15	15	15	15	15	15
16	16	16	16	16	16	16	16	16	16	16	16
17	17	17	17	17	17	17	17	17	17	17	17
18	18	18	18	18	18	18	18	18	18	18	18
19	19	19	19	19	19	19	19	19	19	19	19
20	20	20	20	20	20	20	20	20	20	20	20
21	21	21	21	21	21	21	21	21	21	21	21
22	22	22	22	22	22	22	22	22	22	22	22
23	23	23	23	23	23	23	23	23	23	23	23
24	24	24	24	24	24	24	24	24	24	24	24
25	25	25	25	25	25	25	25	25	25	25	25
26	26	26	26	26	26	26	26	26	26	26	26
27	27	27	27	27	27	27	27	27	27	27	27
28	28	28	28	28	28	28	28	28	28	28	28
29	29	29	29	29	29	29	29	29	29	29	29
30	30	30	30	30	30		30	30	30	30	30
31		31		31	31		31		31		31

COMMENTS/NOTES:

_____

_____

_____

_____

_____

☆ **163** ☆

Ways To Amaze And Engage Middle School Students © 2009 Mar*co Products, Inc. 1.800.448.2197

Name: _____ Grade: _____
                                          Date: _____

Mark with "P" for *Personal* and "G" for *General*

AUG	SEPT	OCT	NOV	DEC	JAN	FEB	MAR	APR	MAY	JUNE	JULY
1	1	1	1	1	1	1	1	1	1	1	1
2	2	2	2	2	2	2	2	2	2	2	2
3	3	3	3	3	3	3	3	3	3	3	3
4	4	4	4	4	4	4	4	4	4	4	4
5	5	5	5	5	5	5	5	5	5	5	5
6	6	6	6	6	6	6	6	6	6	6	6
7	7	7	7	7	7	7	7	7	7	7	7
8	8	8	8	8	8	8	8	8	8	8	8
9	9	9	9	9	9	9	9	9	9	9	9
10	10	10	10	10	10	10	10	10	10	10	10
11	11	11	11	11	11	11	11	11	11	11	11
12	12	12	12	12	12	12	12	12	12	12	12
13	13	13	13	13	13	13	13	13	13	13	13
14	14	14	14	14	14	14	14	14	14	14	14
15	15	15	15	15	15	15	15	15	15	15	15
16	16	16	16	16	16	16	16	16	16	16	16
17	17	17	17	17	17	17	17	17	17	17	17
18	18	18	18	18	18	18	18	18	18	18	18
19	19	19	19	19	19	19	19	19	19	19	19
20	20	20	20	20	20	20	20	20	20	20	20
21	21	21	21	21	21	21	21	21	21	21	21
22	22	22	22	22	22	22	22	22	22	22	22
23	23	23	23	23	23	23	23	23	23	23	23
24	24	24	24	24	24	24	24	24	24	24	24
25	25	25	25	25	25	25	25	25	25	25	25
26	26	26	26	26	26	26	26	26	26	26	26
27	27	27	27	27	27	27	27	27	27	27	27
28	28	28	28	28	28	28	28	28	28	28	28
29	29	29	29	29	29		29	29	29	29	29
30	30	30	30	30	30		30	30	30	30	30
31		31		31	31		31		31		31

COMMENTS/NOTES:

_____

_____

_____

_____

_____

☆ **164** ☆

Ways To Amaze And Engage Middle School Students © 2009 Mar✶co Products, Inc. 1.800.448.2197

Small-Group Evaluation

Purpose:

To have students evaluate a small group in which they participated

ASCA Standards:

PERSONAL/SOCIAL DEVELOPMENT	
Standard A: Students will acquire the knowledge, attitudes and interpersonal skills to help them understand and respect self and others	
PS:A1	Acquire Self-Knowledge
PS:A1.2	Identify values, attitudes and beliefs

Directions:

Review the directions for completing the *Small-Group Evaluation Form*. Collect and tabulate the completed forms.

Ways To Amaze And Engage Middle School Students © 2009 Mar∗co Products, Inc. 1.800.448.2197

SMALL-GROUP EVALUATION FORM

Directions: ***Directions:*** On a scale of 1–5, with 1 being *low,* 3 *average,* and 5 *high,* evaluate our small-group lessons. NA means not applicable. Put an X on the line to evaluate statement.

How did you feel about coming to group?

1.........2.........3.........4.........5   **NA**

How do you feel the students worked together?

1.........2.........3.........4.........5   **NA**

Did you learn new information/skills?

1.........2.........3.........4.........5   **NA**

How well did you trust the group?

1.........2.........3.........4.........5   **NA**

Did you feel other group members listened to you?

1.........2.........3.........4.........5   **NA**

How difficult was it to make up assignments missed while you attended group?

1.........2.........3.........4.........5   **NA**

Would you recommend this group to a friend?

1.........2.........3.........4.........5   **NA**

Are you likely to participate in another group?

1.........2.........3.........4.........5   **NA**

Please list your comments below:

What did you like best about the group? _____
_____
_____

What did you like least? _____
_____
_____

Comments: _____
_____
_____

Ways To Amaze And Engage Middle School Students © 2009 Mar⋆co Products, Inc. 1.800.448.2197

Mediation Contract

Purpose:

To use with students who are experiencing conflict

Materials:

For each student:
- ☐ *Mediation Contract* (page 169 or CD-Rom)
- ☐ Pencil

ASCA Standards:

PERSONAL/SOCIAL DEVELOPMENT	
Standard B: Students will make decisions, set goals and take necessary action to achieve goals.	
PS:B1	Self-Knowledge Application
PS:B1.6	Know how to apply conflict resolution skills
Standard C: Students will understand safety and survival skills.	
PS:C1	Acquire Personal Safety Skills
PS:C1.10	Learn techniques for managing stress and conflict

Directions:

Mediations are conducted between two persons with the help of a mediator.

Begin by asking if each person agrees to the following rules:

1. Don't interrupt.
2. Stay seated.
3. Speak directly to the other person.
4. Work on the problem.

Once they both agree, the mediation may begin.

Have each student tell his/her side of the story, including how it makes him/her feel.

After each person has spoken, the other person repeats what was said. The students may continue, if needed, to discuss the situation.

Ways To Amaze And Engage Middle School Students © 2009 Mar★co Products, Inc. 1.800.448.2197

Have each student state what he/she needs from the other. The mediator writes these statements on the *Mediation Contract,* then reads each statement separately and asks if each person agrees to do what the other persons asks. If they agree, the mediator circles the statement.

Once things are agreed upon, everyone signs the contract.

Each student is given a copy of the signed contract.

Meet with the students in a week to see how things are progressing. Encourage them to contact you if they feel the agreement is not working. The situation may have to be handled by an administrator. Discipline may be involved.

MEDIATION CONTRACT

Each student must agree to the following rules:

1. Don't interrupt.
2. Stay seated.
3. Speak directly to the other person.
4. Work on the problem.

Each student tells his/her side of the story and how what happened made him/her feel.

Each student repeats what the other has said.

Each student states what he/she needs from each other and the mediator writes these needs on the contract.

Mediator circles the things the students agree to do.

The contract is signed.

NEEDS	NEEDS

Student A's signature: _____

Student B's signature: _____

Mediator's signature: _____

Date of contract: _____

Date for contract review: _____
(ONE WEEK FROM DATE OF CONTRACT)

Ways To Amaze And Engage Middle School Students © 2009 Mar*co Products, Inc. 1.800.448.2197

Small-Group Sessions Survey

Purpose:

To identify students who want to be in a group

ASCA Standards:

PERSONAL/SOCIAL DEVELOPMENT	
Standard C: Students will understand safety and survival skills.	
PS:C1	Acquire Personal Safety Skills
PS:C1.5	Differentiate between situations requiring peer support and situations requiring adult professional help

Directions:

Review the information on the *Small-Group Sessions Survey*. Collect the completed surveys and tabulate the results.

SMALL-GROUP SESSIONS SURVEY

Small-group counseling sessions will take place once a week for one class period for approximately 8–10 weeks. If you're interested in participating in one of these groups, please mark your choices below.

Please mark 1 for your first choice, 2 for your second choice, and 3 for your third choice. Return this completed form to the guidance office by _____.

- [ ] **Anger-Management**
- [ ] **Girls' Interest Group**
- [ ] **Divorce Group**
- [ ] **Grab Bag Group**
  (anger-management, stress-management, loss, bullying, and self-esteem)
- [ ] **Loss** (death, moving away, changes)
- [ ] **Self-Esteem**
- [ ] **Ways to Improve in School**
- [ ] **Coping Skills**
- [ ] **Ways to Deal with Stress**

Please list any other group in which you'd like to included.

_____

_____

_____

Name:_____

Grade: _____   Homeroom _____

Ways To Amaze And Engage Middle School Students © 2009 Mar*co Products, Inc. 1.800.448.2197

TOPIC INDEX

☆ **173** ☆

TOPIC INDEX

Ways To Amaze And Engage Middle School Students © 2009 Mar*co Products, Inc. 1.800.448.2197

About The Author

Becky Fesemyer Kirby has been an educator for 37 years, and a school counselor for the past 19 years. Becky works with seventh- and eighth-grade students at Brown Middle School in Ravenna, Ohio. In 2008, Becky was selected as one of the semi-finalists for *American School Counselor Association's Counselor of the Year.*

Becky received an B.S. degree in education from Kent State University. She received a master's degree in school counseling from the same university.

Becky lives in Ravenna with her husband David. Their three children, Kristine, Greg, and Jeff, are all graduates of Ohio State University.

Becky is the author of *Grab Bag Guidance* and *Classroom Guidance From A To Z,* published by Mar*co Products, inc.